Grandfather
KNOWS BEST

Grandfather
KNOWS BEST

Granbill

Contents

Foreword

"Grandfather knows best" reveals a treasure of letters and stories recently discovered nestled on a closet shelf for sixty years.

The letters and stories were written by a grandfather to his first grandchild from the time she was three years old until starting school at age five. He wrote on Sunday afternoons from January 1959 to October 1961.

His pen name Granbill was a combination of Susan's father's name Bill with the prefix gran; in turn, Susan was referred to as Su Su.

The stories are simple and yet intriguing giving way at times to imagination. To illustrate his stories George Price cut out pictures from various magazines and assorted photographs from family activities. The book gives a closeness of family by home gatherings, picnics, holidays and vacations.

You will enjoy the subtle parenting with a soft touch from the distance of a grandparent.

Frank D. Minton

Susan Carey "Su Su"

Susan (Su Su) has been a barber in downtown Oklahoma City for 40 years. She was married just shy of 30 years, until her husband passed away in 2017.

She has five children and eight grandchildren. "I can remember my granbill letting me play with his hair. I would comb it and put clips in it when I was a little girl".

I was his first grandchild and he lived long enough to see all seven of them born. He passed away on my birthday January 18. He was such a kind and gentle man. I have always felt a very strong connection to him.

George O Price author of "Grandfather knows best" was an appliance sales manager at Sears in Wichita, Kansas beginning in 1933 only being interrupted by serving in the Armed Forces during WWII. He died in 1967 at the age of 57 of heart failure.

He is pictured with his eleven year old daughther Jo Anna who, as mother of Susan meticulously saved all the letters her father wrote to Su Su.

Sunday Afternoon
Jan 4 '59

Dear Susie,

I was happy to get your nice letter. I have it along with the others you wrote me in the letter box I received from you for Christmas. Keep writing so I can have a whole box full. Since I can't see you every week letters are the next best thing.

We went to church this morning and saw Rev Crawford. I know you would liked to have seen him. Every time I talk with him he says, "well, well how is Susie getting along?" I miss you too and can hardly wait until you can come to see us and stay a week with us again. Tell Mommie and Daddy hello for me and give Markie a Big kiss for his Grandbill.

Lots of love
Granbill

Su Su Helps Mommie Buy Groceries

One day Mommie said, "Su Su lets go to the grocery store." Susu came running with her pony tail bouncing up and down.

Su Su likes to go grocery shopping with Mommie. She likes to see all the toys at the store. Sometimes Mommie gives her a penny for a ball of gum. Su Su likes to put it in the machine and see the gum come rolling out.

She likes to help Mommie fill her grocery basket,

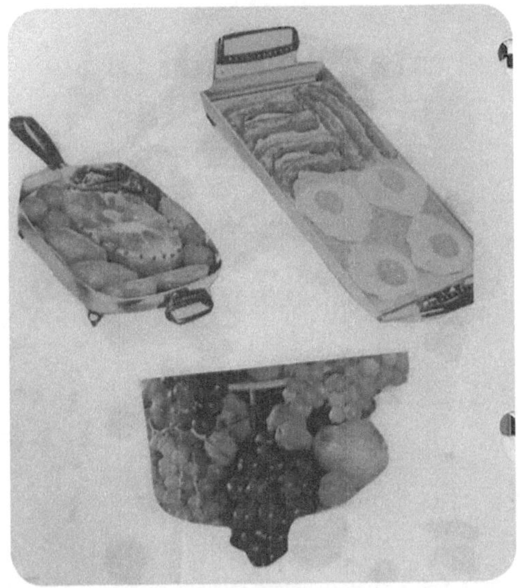

Best of all she is learning how to buy good things to eat and how to be a good cook like mommie.

Every One Loves Su Su

Su Su had a birthday just a week ago. She had three candles on her cake. As she blew them out Grammie thought how nice it would be when Su Su had eight candles on her cake. Then they could go out to dinner together, then go shopping for clothes.

Everyone agrees with Granbill, that Su Su could never be any nicer or sweeter than she is just now, with her sparkling blue eyes, two cute dimples, a bubbling personality a pretty blond ponytail that bobs up and down and a beautiful smile that never quits but goes on and on.

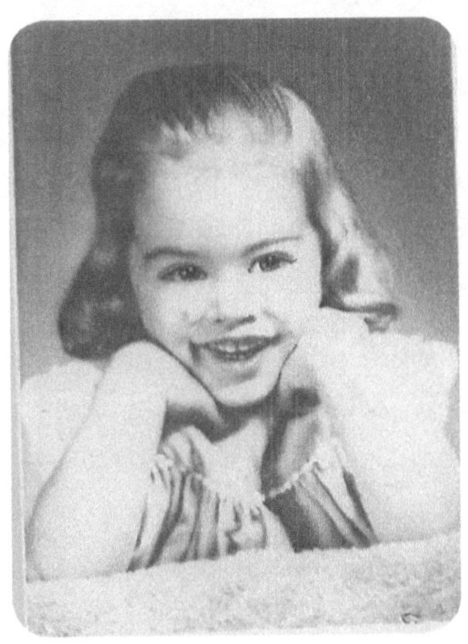

Sunday Eve
Feb 1 '59

Dear Susie,

I wonder if you had a big snow like we have here. It started snowing about noon yesterday and by night we had about eight inches of snow. It sure makes everything look like a beautiful picture. I wish you had been here to help me feed the birds. I cleaned off the snow from the metal table in the yard and put some food on it. The birds flew in and really had a fest. They have to eat good so they will be strong enough to fly.

How is my favorite granddaughter? We would love to see you, Markie, Mommie and Daddy.

Su Su Likes To Eat

Su Su likes to eat good food. She eats cereal, milk, toast, and hot cakes for breakfast but the thing she likes best is bacon and eggs. She likes for Mommie or Daddy to fry them on the grill. Sometimes she eats three or four pieces of bacon and two eggs.

For dinner and supper Su Su eats, fried chicken, ham, vegetables, bread, cake and lots of milk.

Sometimes Su Su thinks it would be nice to have a whole house made of candy and cookies.

Bear Riding

One day Su Su was outside playing and she saw a big bear. The bear said "Hi, Su Su' would you like to take a ride on my back?" Su Su said she would and climbed on the bear's back. Away, they went, the bear going trot trot trit trot with Su Su hanging on for dear life, her ponytail bobbing up and down.

The bear said, "I will take you to my house so you can see my baby bears. Their names are Markie and timmy."

They loved to eat. When Su Su saw them, Markie was eating peanut butter out of the jar and Timmy was pouring milk out of his bottle.

They were so glad Su Su had come to see them; they climbed up in an apple tree and picked some apples for her. The momma bear sat under the tree and caught the apples as they threw them down.

The papa bear's name was Grandbill. He was so glad to see Su Su that he danced a jig. Su Su had lots of fun with the bears. When the bear took Su Su back home, she ran in the house to tell her mommie about visiting the bears, but mommie said "Su Su you know that isn't true." Su Su didn't care because she knew different. She knew she had gone riding on the bear's back.

Sunday Afternoon
Feb 15 '59

Dear Susie

Grammie and I loved the cute Valentines, you and Markie sent. We prize them more than any we ever received. We love you both very much for sending them. We feel so lucky having you and Markie. I am sure we have the most adorable grandchildren in the whole world.

We can hardly wait to see you again. There isn't a day goes by but what I see your picture on the T. V. and say "I want to see my Susie."

We just got home from church and Sunday school.

The weather is so pleasant outside today. It would be nice if you were here to help me rake the yard but not to get a rock on your head again.

Give Mommie and Markie a big kiss for me. Tell your Daddy to let me know when the fish are biting. Maybe we can run down to see your before long.

Love and kisses,
Granbill

Visit Grandbill

When Su Su visits Grambill they have lots of fun. Granbill loves to read to Su Su. They found some stories in a book about Su Su riding the bear's back, Su Su riding the bird's back and Su Su going to the candy store and the candy man made a big candy bar just for Su Su.

Grammie loves for Su Su to visit her too. She made Su Su a snow man cake. It looked like a funny snow man but it tasted delicious with lots of white frosting all covered with coconut.

Airport

Su Su always gets the drumstick when Grammie cooks a turkey. Granbill took a picture of her eating the drumstick of course she couldn't eat it all but it was fun to bite into it.

One day Grammie and Su Su took Granbill to catch a plane. She stood in the airport and waved good bye to him. Granbill liked this very much but he was happier when she was there to meet the plane when he came home to his Su Su. Someday Granbill would like to take Su Su with him on a plane. It would be almost as much fun as riding on the bear's back.

Granbill

Sudnay Afternoon
Feb 22 '59

Dear Susie,

Maybe next Sunday I can visit with you instead of writing. Mommie wrote that you might come to Wichita next week end. I can't think of anything we would rather have than a visit from you.

I saw Rev. Crawford this morning and he wanted to know how Susie was getting along. Maybe you can go to Sunday School with me next Sunday and see him.

We can hardly wait to see Markie with his new haircut. Of course we want to see you, Mommie and Daddy too. We will hope the weather stays nice.

I missed your letter this week but Mommie's letter made up for it, She said you were fine and having fun.

Love and Kisses,
Granbill

Fun at home

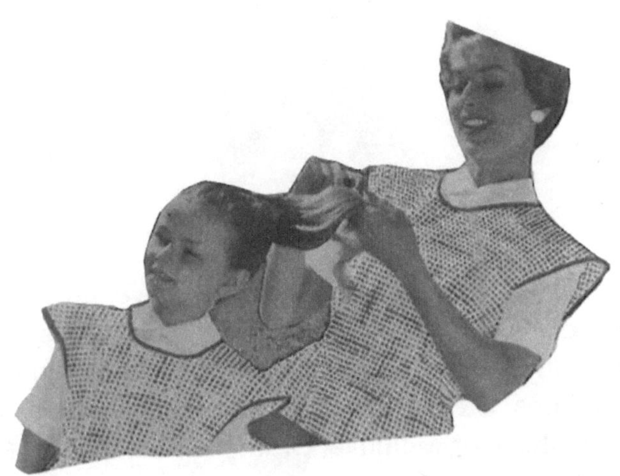

Su Su's day usually starts off with getting her beautiful blond ponytail combed and fixed up by Mommie.

Sometimes Mommie pulls a little, combing but Su Su doesn't complain because she knows all little girls should start their day off by being well groomed, faces clean, hair combed and clean dresses.

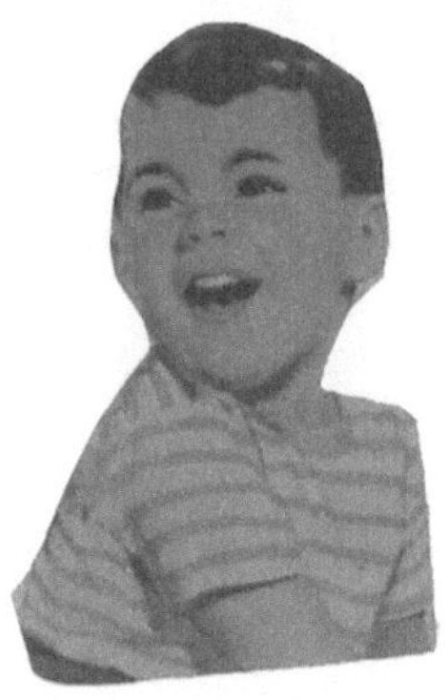

Su Su likes to play with Markie. They have fun playing together. When Mommie is busy and Markie gets cross, Su Su knows just what to do to entertain him. Sometimes Su Su draws pictures for Markie. He thought these of, Mommie, Grammie, Aunt Nancy, and herself were very funny.

Sometimes Mommie and Su Su run down stairs to visit with their friends. While Mommie and her friend have a cup of coffee, Su Su and her friend have a tea party playing they are grown up too

Su Su is a very happy and lovable little girl whether she is visiting at Sunday school or home. She spreads sunshine wherever she goes.

Best of all she has fun.

Sunday Afternoon
Mar 1 '59

Dear Susie,

I am sorry you didn't get to come see me this week but it will be all the nicer when I do see you. If everything turned out the way we wanted them to it wouldn't be as much fun when they do.

I wonder if you went fishing down there. Sure makes me want to get my tackle out and head for the river. Maybe you will take me to your fishing place when I come to see you. Thanks for your letter you sent with Mommies.

I am always glad to hear from you. I am happy Markie is getting along O.K. and that he didn't catch cold over getting his haircut. We miss seeing him and all the rest of you. Tell Mommie we enjoyed her letter very much. It was almost like a visit with you.

Love and Kisses
Granbill

Su Su & Animals

When the three little kittens lost their mittens, it was Su Su who hunted and hunted until she found them, so their mother would give them some pie. Su Su not only found the mittens, she washed them clean and instead of hanging them up to dry, she ironed them until they looked like new. The mother cat was so proud of Su Su she gave her a piece of pie too.

One day a Canary Bird was singing to her babies. She told Su Su she was so tired singing she didn't know what to do. Su Su knew, she got her horn and while the mommie bird sat, she played the babies to sleep.

Dumbo the elephant has a big long nose. Now a big nose is fine in the spring and summer time when it is warm and there are a lot of flowers to smell. In the winter time when the snow is falling and the wind is howling it is a bad thing to have such a long nose. It gets cold as an Icicle. When his nose is cold Dumbo is cold all over. Su Su knew just what to do. She made a glove that looked like a big sock for Dumbo's nose. When she put it on his nose, Dumbo was so warm and snug he thought it was summer again.

Su Su loves all the animals and birds and she is so sweet and kind all the animals and birds love Su Su.

Painting Inside of the House

Su Su has a very pretty home and she loves it. Every one helps keep it clean and shining. When they painted

it, Daddy used a brush and painted the kitchen cabinets. Mommie helped by mixing the paint. Su Su had to watch Markie to keep him from climbing up on the chair and spilling the paint.

Mommie likes to use a roller when she paints the walls. When she was painting the living room, she came very near painting the clock. Su

Su saw her just in time. "No no Mommie," she said. "You don't paint the clock,"

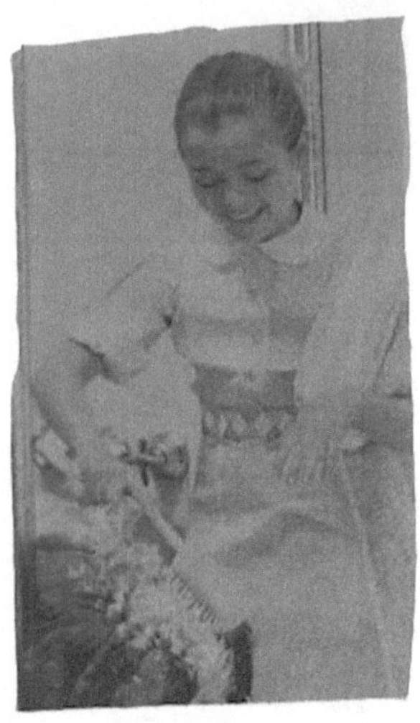

While Mommie and Daddy painted, Su Su got some soapy water and a brush and cleaned the bath room. She scrubbed the walls until they looked just like they had been painted. Markie, came crawling in, to see what Su Su was doing. Before she noticed he wasn't just some more furniture she gave him a scrubbing too.

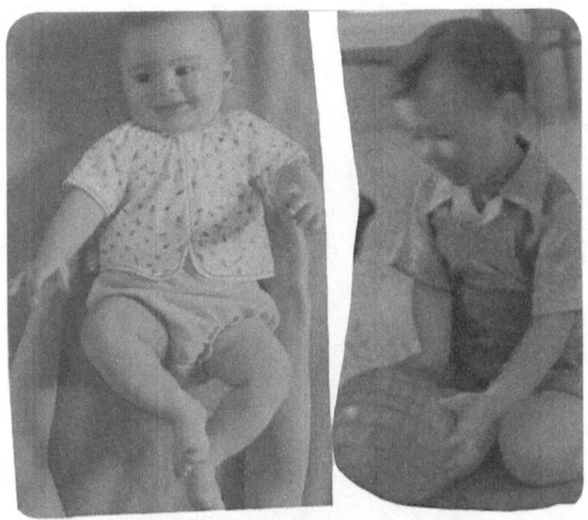

Markie didn't like being scrubbed. He went into the living room and got a ball to play with. As he was playing he was thinking how nice it would be when his little cousin, Timmy would be big enough so they could play ball together. Timmy can hardly wait until he is big enough to play with both, Markie and Su Su.

Swimming

One day when the sun was shining nice and warm, Su Su came running in the house all out of breath. "Mommie Mommie!" she cried, "It is so warm outside,

let's go to the park for a picnic." "O.K. I will fix us a lunch and when Daddy comes home, we will go to the park." Su Su danced with glee. If there is one thing she likes better then ice cream it's going to the park.

Su Su helped Mommie fix the lunch. When

Daddy got home they all went to the park. That is all except Markie. He was in Wichita visiting Grammie and Grandbill. Su Su loved the swings with her Daddy giving her a push she could swing almost as high as the trees. She slid down the slides. She ran and jumped and played so hard she got almost as hungry as the bears in the zoo. The picnic lunch was so good Su Su thought she would never get enough.

After they had all finished eating they stretched out on the cool, green grass and had a good rest. Then Su Su saw the swimming pool. Su Su loves swimming almost as much as going on a picnic. Daddy said, "If we had our suits we would all go swimming."

Su Su is a modest little girl but going swimming is all she heard Daddy say. Even if she had heard more the lack of a suit wouldn't have stopped her.

She shed her clothes in a wink and raced to the pool.
Daddy and Mommie both had a big laugh and Su Su
had a good swim. They went home tired but very happy.

Sunday Night
Apr 4 '59

Dear Susie,

It has sure been lonely around here this week without our Susie. Seems like it has been much longer than a week since we left you in Okla City. I hope you have been having fun. I know Markie, Mommie and Daddy must be happy to have you home.

We went to church this morning. It has been nice and warm here today. I washed both cars. I wished you were here to help me.

I wonder if you went to Sunday School today and maybe to the park this afternoon.

Be sure to write me and tell me what you have been doing and when you are going to come see me again.

Love and Kisses
Granbill

Pop Corn, Chewing Gum, Bubble Gum, Ice Cream Cone, Popsicle, Candy Bar, And Su Su.

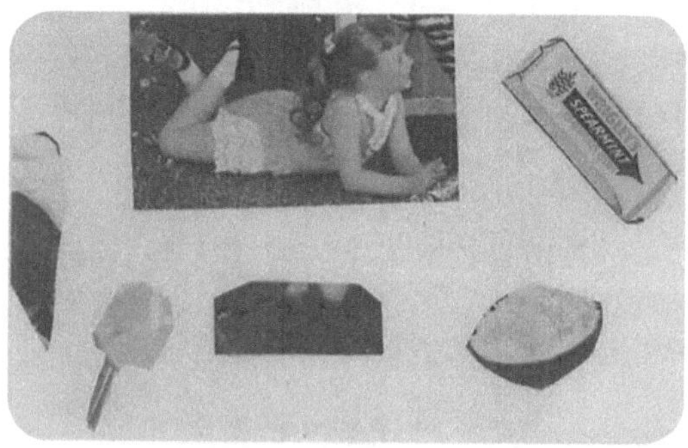

These are the things that made Su Su's visit with Granbill so nice. The popcorn, chewing gum, bubble gum, ice cream cone, popsicle, and candy bar, for Su Su and Su Su for Granbill and Grammie.

Pop Corn, Chewing Gum, Bubble Gum,
Ice Cream Cone, Popsicle, Candy Bar, And Su Su.

Su Su and Granbill had fun working and playing together. Su Su helped Granbill rake the yard. When they got tired they had a tea party.

Su Su made tea and cookies. As they drank tea and ate cookies they planned a fishing trip the next day.

Next day it rained. They couldn't go fishing but they could go to the grocery store. Su Su helped pick out the groceries and push the basket. When they got

home they found they had popcorn, chewing gum, bubble gum, ice cream cones, and candy bars. As Su Su watched, Granbill made some popsicles.

One night, Su Su went to church with Grammie and Granbill. They sat behind Rev. Crawford. Su Su watched him all during the sermon but he didn't see Su Su until church was over. When he turned around and saw her he held out his arms and said. "Well well how is Su Su tonight?"

Sunday Night
April 12, 1959

Dear Susie,

I hear you have been fishing. Better be careful and not catch one big enough to pull you in. It snowed real hard here this morning but it melted about as fast as it fell. Sure looked funny the snow falling on the green trees and grass.

Love and Kisses
Granbill

Su Su Goes Home

When Su Su visited Granbill she was missed by Markie, Mommie and Daddy very much. She is such a happy little girl her laughter makes everyone feel good. Markie missed Su Su most of all. He didn't have any one to play with. Chris the family dog tried real hard to take her place but his bark didn't entertain Markie like Su Su

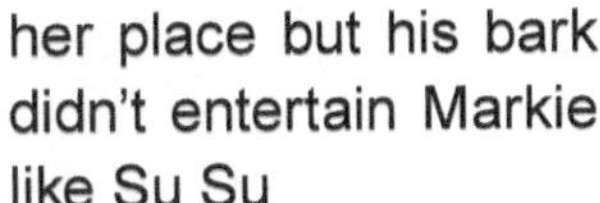

Mommie missed Su Su too because she was so good about helping Mommie.

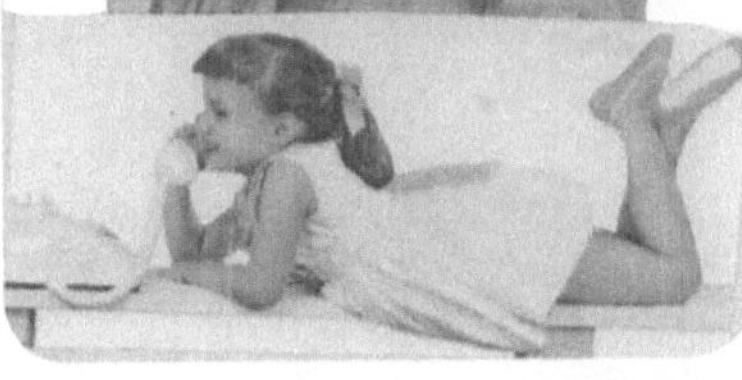

Su Su would pick up Markies toys and help keep the house

straight. She even helped set the table and wash the dishes. When they got the work done Mommie would play telephone with Su Su. They would talk to each other about parties and surprises for Daddy.

Su Su's Sunday school teacher missed her too. She is one of the nicest little girls in the class. She knows just how to do things the way the teacher wants. She plays well with the other children and helps them with their work. Su Su loves her Sunday School and every one loves Su Su.

Daddy missed Su Su too because he didn't have any one to go fishing with. Su Su is a good fisherman. Daddy bought her a fishing outfit, all her own. She can even help bait her own hook.

Fishing

Someday she expects to catch a fish as big as she is. Now that Su Su has gone home, Granbill misses his Su Su too.

Fishing

Sunday Afternoon
Apr 19 '59

Dear Susie,

As I am sitting here writing I see Susie's favorite books. The ones about Su Su riding on the bird's back and the boy with the long nose. How I wish you were here so we could read them together.

We received the cutest pictures of you and Markie today. Sure made us want to see you. Grammie took them to Sunday school today to show off. Everyone thought they were adorable. Of course we agreed with them. I am sure we have the finest Grandchildren in the whole world. We are very proud of our Susie and Markie.

Did you go to Sunday school today? I never go by your Sunday school room here without thinking of you and wishing you were still here so you could go with me.

I just got back from mailing Markie's birthday present and cards. We hope he gets it on his birthday tomorrow. Tell him we are sorry we couldn't be there to help him celebrate.

Love and Kisses
Granbill

Yesterday was one of the biggest events in Markie's life, up till now. He celebrated his first birthday. Mommie baked him a cake. She had it all decorated with one big candle on it. As Mommie, Daddy and Su Su sang "Happy Birth Day, Dear Markie," he tried to blow out the candle. Su Su had to show him how. She knew because she had already had three birthdays. Su Su thinks she is very lucky to have a fine brother like Markie and Markie knows he's very lucky to have a big sister like Su Su.

Fishing

Sunday Night
Apr 25 '59

Dear Susie,

Another week has gone by and it is time to write you again. Can you guess who I would love to see? That is right-my Susie. We just finished our Sunday night hamburgers.

Rev. and Mrs. Crawford came this week and spent the evening with us. Wish you could have been here. They saw your's and Markie's pictures. He thought you both were darling, of course we agreed with him.

The weather has been real nice here today, just right for fishing. I wonder if you went. I spent most of the afternoon working on a chest of drawers.

Sorry Mommie has been sick. Hope she is well now and that you Markie and Daddy escaped having the flu. We hope to see you sometime next month.

Love and Kisses,
Granbill

Mommie

Mommies are wonderful the world over but Su Su thinks she has the most wonderful of all. She is a very pretty Mommie. She has real dark hair, sparkling eyes, a trim little figure and a continuous lovable smile just like Su Su.

Su Su loves to help her Mommie. At night when Mommie gets Markie ready for bed by putting on his sleepers, getting his bottle and blanket ready, Su Su turns down the covers in his bed and then helps him say his prayers.

Su Su helps Mommie take care of Chris. Chris loves mommie too because she is kind to him and feeds him. When Mommie gets busy doing other things, Su Su can take care of Chris almost as good as Mommie.

Mommie shows Su Su how to clean the house and keep it neat. She had Su Su pick up her toys and keep her clothes hung up straight. She is giving Su Su training so that when she gets a home of her own she will know how to keep it nice like Mommie does. Su Su hopes that when she has a little girl of her own she will love Su Su as much as she loves Mommie.

Mommie

Sunday Night
May 3 '59

Dear Susie,

I can hardly wait until next Sunday. I hope then I will
be talking with you instead of writing. We are so glad
you are coming to see us. We received your beautiful
picture yesterday. It looks just like you.

I was glad to get your letter. It is filed away in the letter
box you sent me. If you keep writing I will have to get
me a folder like yours to keep your letter in.

Hope to see you next Sunday,

Love and Kisses,
Granbill

Twins

Blondie, the Mommie cat, had two little kittens just alike. One was called Boots and the other Toots. They had lots of fun playing together. It was real nice most of the time being twins but sometimes it wasn't so good. One day the Mommie cat gave Boots two baths thinking one of the times it was Toots. Another time Toots got two pieces of pie when Mommie thought she was giving each of them one.

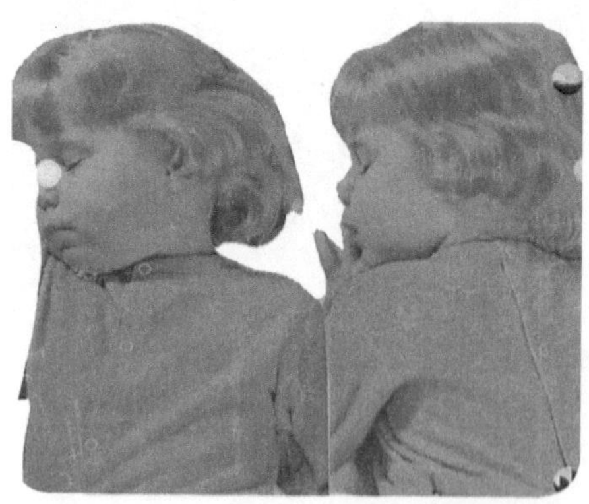

One night Su Su dreamed she became twins. There were two Su Su's and they were exactly alike. They both had beautiful blond hair that Mommie put up in a ponytail. Their eyes sparkled when they laughed and that was most of the time. They were twice as lovable because there was twice as many Su Su's.

Su Su dreamed that Mommie made them each a pretty blue dress. When she dressed them up, Mommie couldn't tell which was which. Daddy came home from work and thought he was seeing double. Markie called them Su Su Thu and Thu Su but he could never tell which was Thu Su and which was Su Thu.

Of course it was all a dream but Granbill wishes there were two Su Su's. One of them could stay with Mommie, Daddy and Markie and the other could live with Grammie, Nancy, Timmy and Granbill. Then Granbill would have a Su Su all his own or would it be Thu Su?

Sunday Afternoon
May 17 '59

Dear Susie,

How is my favorite's granddaughter tday? I can say that now without being partial, since you are the only one I have now, however I am sure if I am lucky enough to have a half dozen others just as sweet as you, you will always have a special spot in my heart.

Did you go to Sunday school this morning? I hope so because you love to go also I am sure you add a lot to your class.

Write me a letter when Mommie has time.

Love and Kisses
Granbill

Spring Time

Su Su loves the springtime, when the sun shines so bright, the grass is soft and green and the flowers dress up in their colorful Easter Bonnets. Su Su and her little friend Rhonda could sit for hours watching the flowers with the butterflys flitting around and the bees gathering honey from the petals.

Su Su loves to go to the park with Mommie, where the leaves are so pretty. She likes to lay in the sun on her Mommies lap and watch the birds flying around in their blue sky.

One day Su Su went out in the country where the flowers grow wild. She was surprised to find them just as beautiful as the ones in the park. The thing she liked best of all was riding a horse. Markie rode up front. He has on his jeans and looked like a real cowboy.

When Su Su walks thru the flowers they all turn their heads to watch her. They enjoy Su Su as much as she enjoys them. When they are all together it is hard to tell which is the more beautiful, the flowers or Su Su.

Spring Time

Sunday Night
May 24 '59

Dear Susie,

It is time I was visiting with you again. That is one of the
best things about Sunday, visiting with you a little while,
even though it is just on paper. It would be much nicer
if I could just drop in at your house for a few minutes or
if you could run over to see Granbill.

I hope you are over your cold and having fun playing.
Tell Mommie and Daddy hello for us and give Markie a
big kiss for his Grammie and Granbill.

Love and Kisses,
Granbill

Two Su Su

Su Su can be the sweetest demure little lady, all dressed up in her pretty bright dresses, here petticoats all starched, and her little pointed toed shoes polished till they shine like glass. With her pretty blond hair in a ponytail, a ribbon on it, she loves to stroll down the street with her Mommie looking like a fashion parade.

Su Su can be a real tomboy when she gets dressed up in her jeans and sneaker shoes. She loves to run and play like a boy. She digs in the sand, gets grass stains on her knees, sand in here hair and dirt on her pretty little button nose. Sometimes she comes in all messed up and Mommie wonders if she will ever get her clean.

Su Su loves dress up parties, fancy cakes, candles, and cookies, colorful balloons, and little girl games. At these parties she is the perfect little lady.

Su Su loves to dress up like a boy, get her fishing pole, a can of worms and go to the lake to fish with her daddy. There she hopes she will catch a fish so big, it will be all she, Markie and Daddy can do to carry it home.

Either as a tomboy or a little lady she is a very pretty lovable little girl.

Sunday Afternoon
May 31 '59

Dear Susie,

How is my best girl today?

I was so glad to get your beautiful picture. You look like a little model. You should go in the business and sell some of them to magazines. I have it in my room so I can say goodnight when I go to bed.

Give Markie a big kiss for us. Give our love to your Mommie and Daddy, and keep a lot for our Susie.

Love and Kisses,
Granbill

Playing Grown Up

Su Su likes to dress up in high heel shoes and grown up dresses. She puts on lipstick and rouge just like Mommie and plays like she is grown up.

Sometimes she pretends she is Mommie sitting out in the yard watching Markie play in his play pen. Markie thinks he is too big to stay penned up. He would rather climb out and play in the dirt and throw mud balls at Su Su.

Sometimes she pretends she is Aunt Nancy with Timmy. Timmy isn't as big as Markie but he is growing fast and in a few more months he and Markie will probably look like twins. When Su Su thinks how cute Markie and Timmy are she had just as soon be big sister and older cousin.

One time when Su Su saw a Mommie cat playing with her kittens she thought it would be nice to be a mommie cat and have such cute kittens. Whether she is watching Mommie and Markie or Mommie cat and her kittens, Su Su is learning so that when she is old enough to be a Mommie, her children will think she is the best little Mommie in the world.

Sunday Afternoon
June 7, 1959

Dear Susie,

I wonder what you are doing today. We are just being lazy. Grannie and I went to Church and Sunday School.

After dinner we turned on the air conditioner and have been just lying around enjoying it.

I hear you have been going to Bible School. I think that is real nice. How much longer will it last? It looks now we won't get to see you two weeks from today at Enid.

How is Markie? We are getting anxious to see him too. Tell Mommie and Daddy we would love to see them also.

Love and Kisses,
Granbill

Zoo Visit

Next to popcorn, chewing gum, candy bars and popsicles, Su Su likes to go to the park and visit the zoo. There she buys a sack of popcorn and shares it with the ducks and geese. When they see Su Su they say "Quack! Quack! Here comes Su Su. We love Su Su, she feeds us. Quack! Quack!"

Su Su saw another bird too. It was much smaller than the ducks and geese but it was more beautiful. Its grey, green and black feathers shone like silk. It's pretty red beak nestled in a little puff of feathers peeked through like a ripe cherry. It was a Parakeet. It not only talked but when Su Su went by it whistled wheeeeee Wheeet!

Su Su loves the big tiger too. It looks a lot like a kitten but is much more fierce and larger. It can roar almost as loud as a lion. He wears a pretty golden coat with black stripes around it. His whiskers are white and his eyes are green. The tiger loves Su Su too and when she asks it he will jump a hoop for her.

The thing Su Su likes best about the park and zoo is the buggy ride. A beautiful pony takes her riding around the park in a rubber tired buggy. As she passed by Mommie she waved to her and Mommie took some movies of Su Su in the buggy. Su Su loves all the other animals too and will visit them next time.

Sunday Afternoon
June 14 '59

Dear Susie,

This time next Sunday I should be with my Susie. I can hardly wait, can you? We hope the weather will be nice so we can have a picnic outside also I want to get some movies too. Tell your Mommie and Daddy they would probably like to bring their camera too.

I haven't heard whether you are planning to come home with me from Enid. I am sure Mommie will write us this week and let us know. We are looking forward to having you but if for any reason you can't come we will understand.

See you next Sunday.

Love and Kisses
Granbill

Bed Time

Helping Mommie playing with Markie and all the other activities of a little three and a half year old girl leaves Su Su tired out at the end of the day. She likes to sit around with Mommie, Daddy and Markie, eating popcorn, and just being pretty.

When Mommie says "Su Su it is time for bed" Su Su gets into her pajamas, She kisses Daddy, Mommie and Markie good-night and then goes to her own bed, says her prayers. She gets a good night's sleep so she will be fresh and rested for a new busy day, tomorrow.

Sometimes Su Su helps Mommie get Markie ready for his bed. She gets his blanket for him and finds a little bunch of fuzz for Markie to rub his nose with so he can go to sleep.

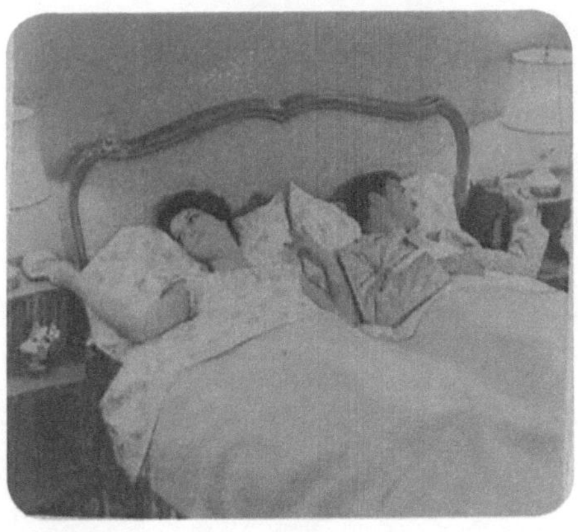

Sometimes Markie and Su Su both wake up in the morning before Mommie and Daddy do. They tiptoe into their room and before they know what has happened, Su Su and Markie land right in the middle of the bed with Mommie and Daddy. They awake with a start but are happy to see two bright happy faces, ready for another busy day.

Sunday Night
July 12 '59

Dear Susie,

It has only been a week since we took you home. We have missed you a lot but you left us some very pleasant memories of the things you said and did while you were here. There is hardly a day goes by but what someone quotes Susie. Then someone says lets have some pop kern. So you see even though you are at home with Mommie and Daddy we still have part of you here. I hope the next time you come nothing else happens like a rock on your head or chicken pox.

It seems your sweet personality, your humor, and quaint speech was more contagious than your chicken pox.

Love and Kisses
Granbill

Su Su Being Self

Su su could never be any lovelier or sweeter than she is just now. But like grown up people she sometimes wishes she were different. There are times when she would like to be a little older. She could put on her own pretty party dress and fix her own hair with a ribbon instead of ponytail.

Other times when she, Markie, Mommie, and Daddy are out in the yard, playing together, she thinks it would be nice to trade ages with Markie. She would be the little sister and Markie would be the big brother.

Su su loves picnics with Mommie, Daddy and Markie. They have lots of fun and good things to eat. One time at a picnic, for no reason, Su Su found herself wishing she had short black hair instead of her blond ponytail.

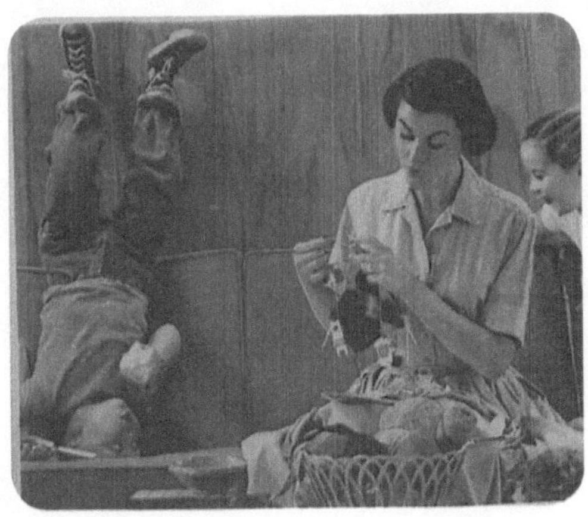

But in the evening, after the dinner dishes are done. Mommie gets out her sewing. Su Su is glad she is being taught how to sew by Mommie, instead of Markie, in his blue jeans standing on his head.

If Su Su Had Been Born South Of The Border

When Su Su goes to school she will learn about neighbors who live , not just across the street , or next door but just the next country South. If Su Su had been born in Mexico, chances are, her name would have been Lolita instead of Su Su. Her skin would have been much darker and instead of pushing a button to turn on the lights she might have to use candle.

If Markie had been born in the country justy South, his name might have been Manuel and he would say "Si Si" instead of yes yes. He would wear a broad brim straw hat, baggy trousers and over his shoulders or around his waist, what looks like a small blanket but is called a serape. His dark skin and jet black hair would make him a quaint looking little fellow.

Even though their skin might have been darker and their dress different, Manuel and Lolita would have the same feelings as Su Su and Markie. They would enjoy playing the same games, laugh at the same things, and be loved by their Daddy and Mommie just like Su Su and Markie.

Being brother and sister, Lolita and Manuel would love each other just as much as Su Su and Markie love each other. They would enjoy playing together, they might quarrel with each other a little but they would stand up for each other against anyone else. They would probably eat taco's instead of hamburgers but regardless of race or color little boys and girls are pretty much the same world over.

Sunday Afternoon
July 19 '59

Dear Susie,

Another week has gone by and it is time to write my Susie a letter.

Grammie and I are all alone. She is reading the Sunday papers while I write you. It would be nice to have you here to keep us company.

It has been real cool here this week. I wonder if it has been warm enough there for you to go swimming. Have you been back to the park since we were there? We thought it was a very nice park. We enjoyed watching you ride the Merry-go-round, the little cars and air planes. We have a place like that here. Maybe we can take you there when you come so see us again. Will you try not to take the chicken pox or get sick the next time? So we can go more places and do more things for you.

How are you doing on candy bars? We haven't had a bite of pop kern since you were here. Give our love to Markie, Mommie and Daddy, and keep a lot for your self.

Love and Kisses,
Granbill

Su Su, Markie & Timmy

Su su is a very happy little girl. She enjoys most any kinds of play and some kinds of work. The thing she likes best of all is going swimming. Mommie helps her into her bathing suit, rubs on sun-tan lotion and Su su is ready for a big splash in the pool.

Su Su's little brother, Markie, is too small to work. He likes to pull Su Su's hair. He loves his blanket and almost purr's likes a kitten when he rubs it over his nose. He is happy most of the time. The thing he likes to do best of all is to get into Mommie's cabinets. There he pulls out the pans bangs them together, turns over the garbage can and scatters paper all over the floor.

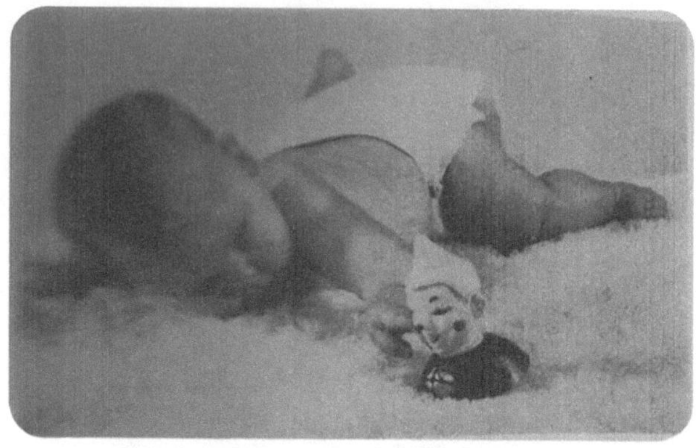

Su su's little cousin, Timmy, is younger than Markie but he is learning to crawl. He gets into everything he can reach. He loves to eat his vegetables and drink milk from a bottle. The thing he likes best of all is a roly poly toy clown Su Su gave him. He rolls it over and it comes back upright, causing him to bubble with laughter.

At the close of a busy day Su Su loves to cuddle and listen to Mommie read about the adventures of other little girls, boys and animals. She loves to hear of the nice things that happen to them. But she knows that having Mommie, Daddy Markie and a little cousin Timmy makes her the luckiest little girl of all.

Granbill

Sunday Afternoon
July 26 '59

Dear Susie,

It was nice to get your letter. I enjoyed it very much. You will have to write more often. I think Grammie enjoyed it almost as much as I did. We look forward to both yours and Mommie's letters. It is almost like a visit with you.

I hope you like the swimming pool we sent you. It is more like a sitting pool isn't it? I know it is too small for a big girl like you. Since you don't have an elephant in your back yard to give you a shower, maybe you can cool off in it when the weather is hot.

Love and Kisses,
Granbill

Visiting Granbill

Su Su's Granbill thinks she is about the finest little Granddaughter any one ever had. It is hard to tell who has the most fun when Su Su visits him. Su Su loves to take a shower bath under the garden hose. One day she turned the hose on Granbill and he almost jumped out of his skin when the cold water hit him but Su Su just laughed at him.

Su Su helps Granbill when he mowed the lawn. She picks up sticks, grass and leaves. Su Su is careful not to pick up rocks. She remembers how one day she threw one up in the air and it came down on her head. Now she only picks up soft things like grass and leaves, and saves the rocks for Grandbill.

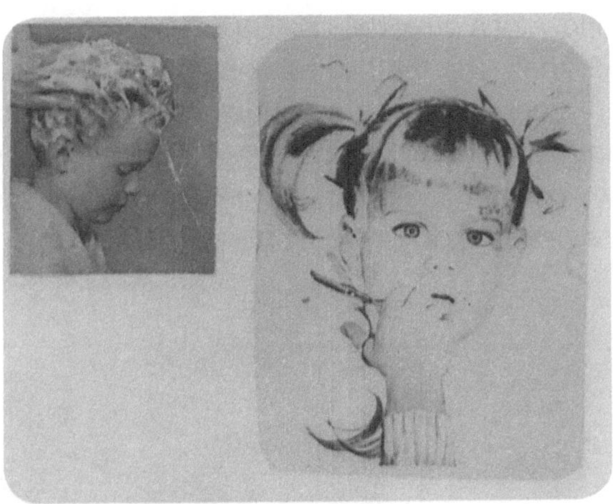

Even at Granbill's, Su Su gets her weekly shampoo to keep her pretty blond hair clean and shining. Grammie rubs the shampoo in good and rinses it out. Su Su keeps her eyes shut tight. She likes soap in her hair, not in her eyes. Su Su didn't think Grammie fixed her hair just right so she trimmed it to suit herself.

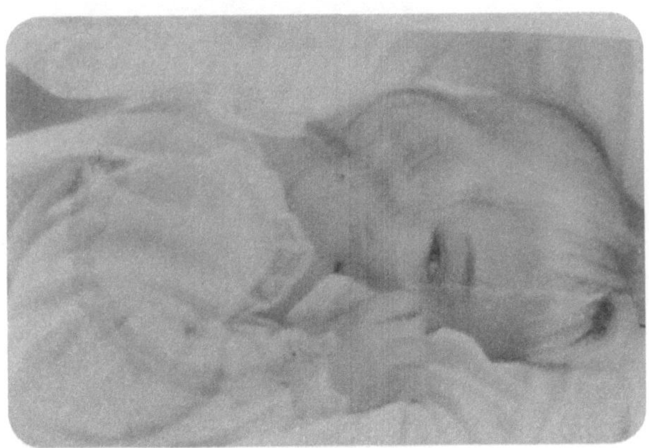

At the close of a busy day, Su Su loves to go to bed and have Granbill scratch her back as she goes to sleep. She dreams of another busy day tomorrow with new adventures, laughter and maybe a few tears, but never a dull moment. It is all part of a little girl growing up as she lives each new day to its fullest.

Su Su's Mommie keeps busy too with her Su Su and Markie. Of course Su Su is big enough to keep out of mischief and helps mommie's look out for Markie. But one day when Mommy was talking on the phone, Su Su just couldn't resist showing him how to eat jelly with her hands. Mommies are busy people but they love it when they are busiest because then they know that their Markie and Su Su's are healthy and happy.

Aug 16 '59

Dear Susie,

I am getting real anxious to see you. If your vacation didn't start in another three weeks, I would be tempted to come see you next week. But maybe I can wait. We bought a ham and will have it in the freezer waiting for your visit. I also went fishing last Tues and caught two catfish. One weighed four pounds and the other four and one half. I think we will have some of them left by the time you come. I will try to have some popsicles made up just for my Susie. Grammie is watching T.V.

I guess you had company today, hope you had fun playing with the twins. I wonder if you could tell them apart. It's too bad you aren't twins so one of you could stay with me, but I guess it would be hard to choose between Su Thu and Thu Su I would probably want both of you.

Love and Kisses,
Granbill

One day when Su Su and Markie were out playing they were surprised to see a car full of small elephants drive up. There was Mommie elephant, Daddy elephant and little Dumbette. They were so small Su Su could hardly tell they were elephants. Little Dumbette wasn't much larger than her dog Chrisie. He said he had come to play with Su Su and Markie.

Most elephants are very large, with ears the sizes of Markie's blanket. If they are not in zoos, they live in a country far away, all except Su Su's little Dumbette. One day when Su Su was at the zoo, she gave an elephant some peanuts. He loved Su Su and said he would have his little grandson, Dumbette come see her.

Su Su and Markie had lots of fun playing with little Dumbette. They played ball. They laughed when little

Dumbette caught and threw the ball with his nose. He used his nose, called a trunk, just like Su Su used her hands. It was almost dark when little Dumbette said he had better go home. Su Su wanted to call his Mommie but he said, "No, I can find my way home." But he couldn't, he got lost. All the houses looked alike. He was so small he couldn't see around or over them to see where he lived.

A kind policeman found little Dumbette wandering around tired, hungry and crying. It was only few minutes before the policeman located the little elephant's home. Dumbette was never so happy to see his home. The ice cream the policeman had bought him never tasted so sweet before. He told the policeman how he had enjoyed playing with Su Su and Markie. Dumbette's Daddy was glad to see the policeman and thanked him for bringing his little son home. Little Dumbette visits Su Su often and they have lots of fun but Su Su calls his Mommie when it is time to go home.

Sunday Afternoon
Aug 2 '59

Dear Susie,

It is hot enough here to go swimming but since we don't have a pool, I will sit by the air conditioner and write my Susie. We were glad to get your's and mommie's letters. They help us from missing not having you close enough to run and see us every day or two.

Glad you are enjoying your swimming pool. What happens to the water when you and Markie all get in it at one time? It doesn't seem as if there would be any room for water when you are all in it. Maybe next year we can trade that one in for a larger one.

Thanks for the pictures you and Mommie sent. Maybe I can find a story about Su Su in them. You know Su Su is such a very busy little girl that I sometimes have a hard time finding pictures to show what all she does. Mommies are busy too as you will see in Su Su's story this week.

Love and Kisses,
Granbill

Su Su is an unusual sweet girl but sometimes she slips a cookie from her Mommies cookie jar and gets sugar all over her mouth. Even trying to look like a little angel the sugar trace gives her Mommie a smile and a no-no look.

Sunday
Aug 29 '59

Dear Susie,

I probably won't be writing you next Sunday because you should be here just one more week until your vacation starts. I can hardly wait to see you. I wonder if you were going to bring Chris to visit him. Timmy said he wanted to see his cousins, SU SU, and Markie. He has his first tooth to show off. I bet you will think he has grown a lot since you last saw him.

Grammie and I found somethings at the grocery store we think you will like. Let's hope the days go by quickly so you will be here soon.

Love and Kisses,
Granbill

Billy the goat is a tough, stubborn and sometimes dull animal. Billy loves Su Su and tries very hard to please her. She hitches him up to her wagon like a pony and he pulls her around the block. What Billy can't do by himself is to always smell as sweet as a daisy. Su Su knows what to do though, she just sprinkles him with her Sachet.

Billy is a watch dog for Su Su. When Su Su tries to get too close to the Lilly pond pool in the backyard he stands like a guard in front of it. When Su Su tries to go around Billy he gently butts her away. Su Su laughs!

Shep the dog and Markie Duck are not natural friends, but because they both Love Su Su, they play together and are not afraid of each other. Sometimes Markie Duck wanders away into the street. Shep is always watching over him and will pick him up very carefully carrying back to the yard, so he won't get hit by a car.

One of the things that keeps Mommies busiest is keeping watch so her youngsters won't get hurt or into mischief. One day when the Mommie fox wasn't looking Timmy fox chased some birds. He was having the most fun, he thought, until the Mommie bird saw him and flew down and pecked him on the nose. Timmy ran crying to his mommie, She wiped his tears away and kissed his nose and he was happy again.

Mommies Are Busy People

One day when Su Su saw a mommie cat with her kittens she thought, how busy people mommies are. The mommie cat is kept busy all day caring for her kittens. She watches to keep them out of the street, feeds them, washes their faces and tucks them in bed at night.

Mommie foxes are busy too. Su Su thinks they look like cousins of her dog Chris.

The mommie fox takes her two little ones for a walk through the woods. She teaches them how to hunt for their food and where to find delicious grapes that they love, like Su Su loves ice cream and pop kern. The Mommie fox calls her youngsters Timmy and Markie.

Sunday Eve.
Sept 27 '59

Dear Susie,

It is now seven O'clock Sunday eve, and time to write my Susie. It was so nice to see you and visit with you this week. We enjoyed every minute of it, thanks to you, Markie, Mommie and Daddy.

I wonder if you went to church and Sunday school today as we did. I bet you were at Sunday school if not Church.

We are hoping we can have you come stay with us for a week or so this fall. You think about it and try to decide when would be the best time. Tell your Mommie and Daddy we will try not to spoil you too much.

Love and Kisses,
Granbill

Dog Friends

Dogs are Su Su's favorite animal friends. She loves her dog Chris and Chris loves Su Su. She has seen many other nice dogs and would like to keep them all but she knows there isn't enough room in her yard and house for more than one and she would rather have Chris.

Some dogs remind Su Su of little girls. They get all perfumed up; have their hair shampooed and curled some even have ribbons in their hair. When they get all dressed up they wouldn't think of getting out and playing in the dirt. They strut around like a little girl in can can petticoats.

Some dogs remind Su Su of her little brother, Markie. They are not too particular about staying clean. They are a little wobbly on their legs. Some have big feet but they are friendly and lovable. They just love to roll around in the grass and mud.

Other dogs are like Su Su. They stay clean and smelling sweet all the time. They love to play and have fun. They even like ice cream. They are most like Su Su because they are always friendly, lovable and love all their other little animal friends.

Sunday Afternoon
Oct 11 '59

Dear Susie,

I was glad to get your good letter. It was almost like visiting with you. You write real well, almost as good as Mommie, in fact it looks a lot like hers.

Grammie and I are sitting here wishing we could see our Oklahoma families. We got the movies back we took while at your house. They are real good, some of you in your ladies dress up clothes, and of your pretty home.

Love and Kisses,
Granbill

Mommie, Su Su and Markie love for daddy to paint their home. He painted the living room, the kitchen and their bedrooms. Mommie liked her room the best but Su Su and Markie thought theirs were the prettiest.

Su Su likes to paint but she couldn't understand why Mommie didn't like it when Su Su painted Markie.

Su Su is very thankful for good food. When she sits down at the table to eat, she says a Blessing. She gives Thanks for all the different kinds of food on the table, for her happy home, for Mommie, for Daddy and for her little brother, Markie.

Su Su loves a good breakfast. She knows it will make her strong and healthy. She also knows where the food she likes comes from. The milk she drinks comes from beautiful cows. They eat grass and grain that grows in the sunshine and makes it into milk for Su Su. When she drinks her milk she is also drinking a little bit of sunshine.

The orange juice Su Su likes so well doesn't grow in cans that she gets it from but is taken from beautiful golden oranges. They grow on trees where the sun shines a lot. The oranges are first beautiful flowers that Su Su loves to smell and that bee's gets honey from. Su Su loves honey the bees make, so she really gets oranges, honey and orange juice from the same trees.

The Elephant

One of the animals that Su Su likes best, when she visits the zoo, is the elephant. Of course they get much larger than the one Su Su has by the ear. Even the little ones have ears as big as Markie's blanket. Su Su thought, if Markie's nose was a big as the elephants, Markie would need a much larger blanket to rub it with when he goes to sleep.

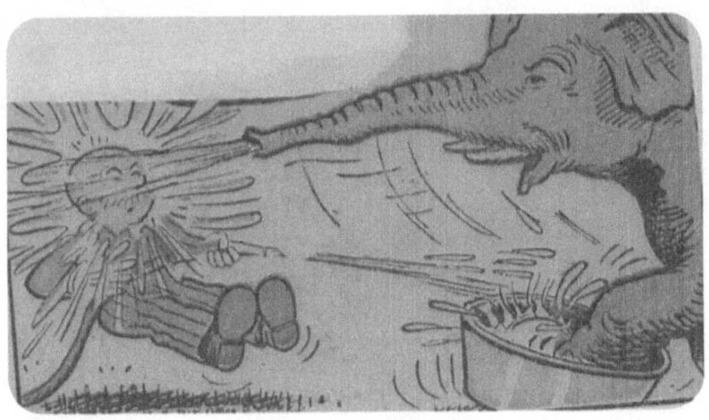

The elephant's nose is called a trunk. Su Su doesn't know why because it looks more like a long sock. The elephant uses his trunk like Su Su uses her hands. He picks up things with it, uses it to put food in his mouth and can even give people a shower bath with it. Su Su thought it would be nice to have him in her back yard when it gets hot, then Mommie wouldn't have to get out the water hose to give Su Su a shower.

An elephant has a good memory. He doesn't forget nice things people do for him. The elephant always remembers Su Su because she gave him some of her pop kern which he loves very much. He has a very small tail for such a large animal. Su Su thought maybe part of it was used to make his trunk.

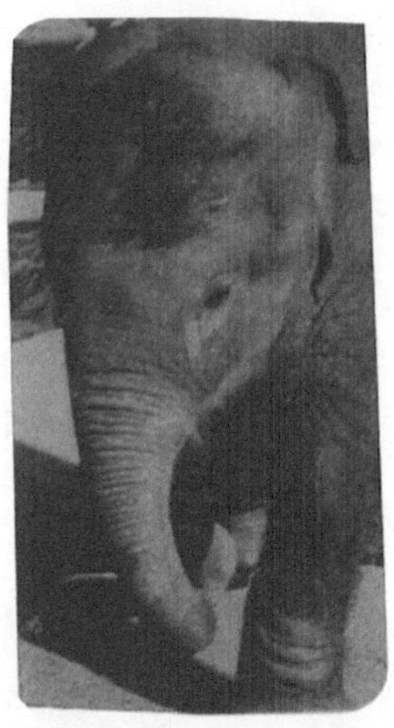

Su Su likes the elephant but she wouldn't like to be one because when they get older they get so large they can't sit or lay down. If they did they couldn't get up. They even have to sleep standing up. Su Su would much rather lay down to sleep in her soft bed.

Su Su loves to sit at her window and look outside at the beauty Mother Nature paints. The beautiful green of the trees, the flowers of all shades of pink, blue, yellow, white and red, the blue sky and the white clouds. They all blend together to make a beautiful picture.

Sunday Eve.
Oct 18 1959

Dear Susie,

I am counting the Sundays until you come to see me. If you come the second Sunday of November, which will be the eighth, it will be just four Sundays from today. Will you ask Mommie if the date is right?

We have a Special Service at the Church next Sunday afternoon, we are obligated to attend. We will probably wait now until you come up here. I hope you like the story about the little Drumbette.

We think Nancy and Timmy might decide to come for Thanksgiving. We will try to have a big turkey. Guess who will get the drum stick, do you think you will be able to eat a whole one?

Love and Kisses,
Granbill

Sunday Night
Oct 25 '59

Dear Susie,

It was nice to talk to you on the telephone last Sunday. You sounded like a big girl. If you have grown as much as you sounded on the phone you must be almost as tall as Mommie.

It will only be three more weeks until you come. Are you counting the days as I am? I will try to have some candy bars ready when you come. Are you going Trick or Treating Halloween? I wish you could knock on my door. I would try to fill your sack.

Tell Markie, Mommy and Daddy we would like to see them too. Are you taking good care of Markie? I think they are lucky to have Su Su all the time. They should share more with me.

Love and kisses,
Granbill

A Carnival

Su Su loves a carnival; the Merry-go-round, the swings, the airplane and boat rides. She loves the crowds of people and to hear the happy laughter of other little boys and girls. Su Su also likes the popcorn and peanuts her Daddy buys her when they go to the park and carnival.

Markie likes carnivals too. One day he dressed up like an Indian. He got on a Merry-go-round pony and rode it around yelling and whopping it up with great excitement. Su Su laughed when she saw a little dog barking back at him.

Next to the carnival in the park Su Su likes the swimming pool. She likes to see the boys and girls dive and splash in the pool. Someday Su Su hopes she can learn to swim as fast as the fish she saw in a pool at the park.

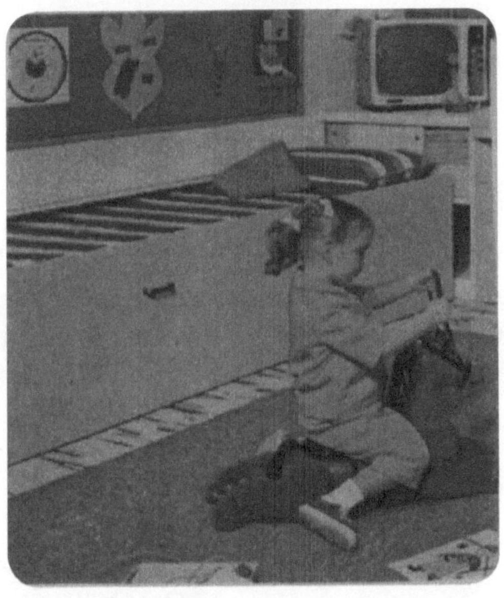

Sometimes Markie and Su Su play Carnival at home. Su Su gets on Markie's horse and pretends she is riding a Merry-go-round. Markie uses the swing in his yard to make believe he is riding the Carnival airplanes. Markie and Su Su both had a big laugh when their dog Chrisie tried to roar like a lion in the zoo.

Sunday Eve
Nov 1 '59

Dear Susie,

I enjoyed your nice letter very much. It sounded just like you talk. Thanks for the pictures they will help me with some Su Su stories. Did you have fun playing Trick or Treats? I bet you got more than you could eat.

It won't be long till you will be coming to Wichita. I am counting the days until then. I can hardly wait to see those new shoes you have. Be sure to wear them when you come. I have some film left in the movie camera to take your picture. We need yours and Markie to finish the roll.

It is time for bed. By for now.

Love and kisses,
Granbill

Happy for all Seasons

Su Su is a happy little girl. She loves every minute of every day and every day of every season of the year. She finds something special for each season. The spring brings green grass and lovely flowers. After the cold winter days and staying inside by the fire Su Su can hardly wait to get outside and help the grass push through and the flowers to bloom.

After Spring comes Summer. The days are longer and warmer. With Summer comes picnics, fishing and visits to the park and zoo with Mommie, Daddy and Markie. At the park Su Su loves to ride the Merry-go-round, the swings, boats and airplanes. The zoo is where Su Su sees all her animal friends. They all love Su Su. The thing Su Su loves best of all in the Summer is swimming at the pool.

Su Su is happy in the fall too. She loves the beautiful trees and shrubs as they dress up in their fall finery. Their leaves are more colorful than the paint Su Su has in her color book. Best of all she loves Halloween. She dresses up in funny clothes and a mask and goes Trick or Treating.

After fall Su Su looks forward to winter. Again the whole outdoors changes color, as the beautiful snow sifts down leaving everything covered in a white blanket as soft as down. Su Su loves to make snow men and throw snowballs. Winter also has something real special for Su Su. She knows the snow brings Christmas. Everything brings happiness to Su Su and Su Su brings happiness to everyone.

Animals & People

Some animals remind Su Su of people she has seen and knows. She saw three beautiful cats after their baths; so clean looking so colorful, their fur as soft as feathers and was reminded at once of three little girls.

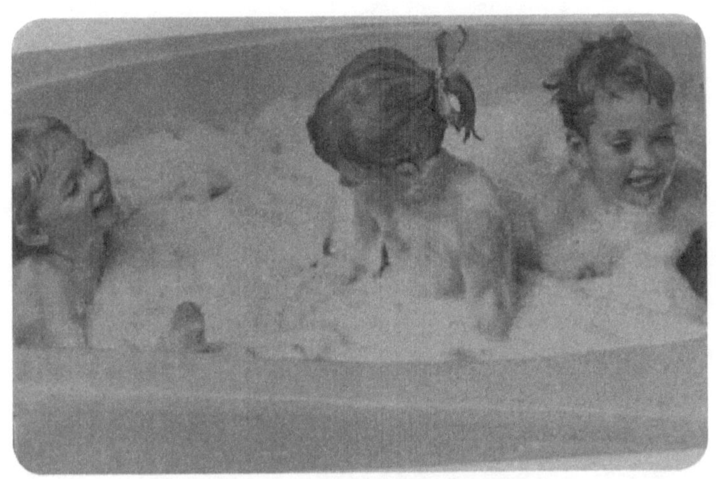

These little girls were taking a bubble bath. Their faces as soft as the kittens fur. They were so beautiful they all looked like Su Su. Their names were Thu Su, Su Thu, and Chu Thu.

Another animal Su Su loves is called a woodchuck. A Woodchuck is a happy little animal. He loves the Springs, the Summers and the Fall of the year when the weather is warm and mild. He romps and plays in the green grass. The WoodChuck is such a cute, loveable little bundle of fur. He reminds Su Su of her little cousin Timmy, when he sits up on his haunches and wrinkles up his nose.

Sunday Eve
Dec 6 '59

Dear Susie,

How is my best girl? I have missed you this week. We went to another wedding today, you would have enjoyed. It was a red and white wedding. The bridesmaids wore red and the bride and bridegroom white. The little taper lighter could only get three candles lighted. The others were too high for her to reach. Too bad you couldn't have been the flower girl.

Mr. Jack & Reddy

Mr. Jack Rabbit is a happy fellow. He hops around in the sunshine on the green grass. He doesn't have much to worry about. When he is hungry he just eats the grass all around him. When he is sleepy he merely hops over to the shade of a shrub and the grass makes him a soft mattress. He sleeps just as soundly as Su Su does on her soft bed. There is one thing though, Mr. Jack has to watch out for and that is Reddy Fox.

Reddy has a mean streak in him when it comes to rabbits. He not only loves to chase rabbits, if he catches one he eats it for his dinner. When he saw Mr. Jack hopping along he decided to have some fun and dinner. Mr. Jack wasn't caught napping. When he saw Reddy coming, he stretched out running lickity-split. His ears laid back like the handlebars of Su Su's tricycle. Mr. Reddy was a little faster and that would have been the end of Mr. Jack if it hadn't been for Su Su.

Su Su saw Mr. Jack's plight, just as two beautiful hound dogs came by. "Go get Reddy Fox," She told them. Off they went barking and bellowing every jump. Now it was Reddy's turn to be frightened. He forgot all about Mr. Jack and begin to run for dear life. He knew if the dogs caught him they would do to him what he planned for Mr. Jack.

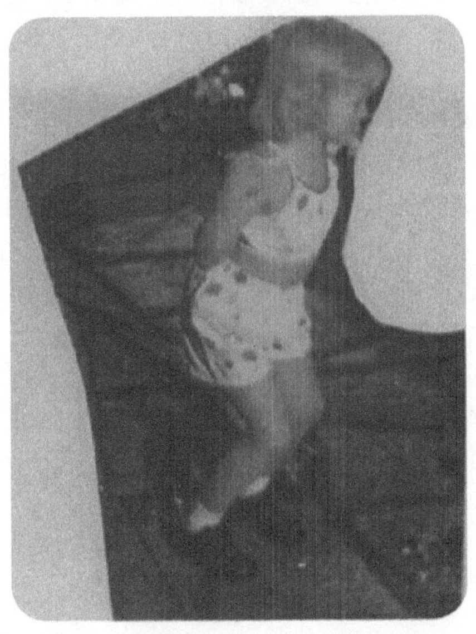

Now Su Su is such a kind little girl she didn't want any of her animal friends hurt. Just as the dogs were about to catch Reddy, she called to them. "Stop; don't hurt Reddy!" She knew Reddy had learned his lesson, what it is to be chased by someone larger than he is. The dogs let Reddy go. Su Su was glad. The dogs had saved Mr. Jack and she saved Reddy.

Sunday Afternoon
Dec 13 '59

Dear Susie,

If the next week goes as fast as the last one it won't be long until you come to see me again. Do you know it is only twelve more days until Christmas. Grammie is wrapping packages now and we want to get them all mailed by Tuesday. We will keep yours here and that way you will have to wait until Christmas to open them, unless you come here sooner. Do you have your tree up yet? I bet you will have a hard time keeping Markie wanting to open the package. I bet you had fun riding Santa's sleigh at Sears. Did you tell him what you want for Christmas?

Give our love to your Mommie, Daddy, and Markie, and keep a lot for yourself.

Love and kisses,
Granbill

The Days

This has been a short busy year for Su Su. It only seems a few weeks ago that it was spring. The grass had just come up, out of the ground, where it had been all winter to keep warm. The flowers were putting on their beautiful spring bonnets like Su Su at Easter.

Then came summer and with it some of Su Su's happiest days. Swimming, going to the park, riding the merry-go-round, the swings, the slides, going fishing, picnics, ice cream, popsicles, it was over all too soon.

Next came fall. Again the trees, flowers, and shrubs, put on another change of color. Some of them shed their leaves to make a blanket that keeps their feet warm when the snow comes. Su Su had lots of fun trick and treating. She loved the cool evenings in her home by the warm stove with Markie, Daddy and Mommie popping corn and reading books.

Now Su Su is looking forward to the most thrilling time of the year. It is getting colder. Already some snow has fallen and Su Su knows who loves snow: the fat, jolly, little man with a bag full of toys and a sled pulled with reindeers. It can mean only one thing, Christmas will soon be here.

Sun Night
Dec 20 '59

Dear Susie,

We have lots of packages around our Christmas tree and several of them have your's and Markie's name on them. I am sure you will have a big Christmas and by the time you get this letter it will only be two more days until you come to see me.

Love and kisses,
Granbill

Su Su Helps Mommie Robbin

One day Su Su looked out her window and saw mommie Robbin feeding her babies. She thought the babies looked funny with their necks stretched out and their mouths opened so wide they could have swallowed each other. When it is summer time mommie Robbins can find worms and seeds to feed her babies but when the snow covers everything, Su Su takes bread crumbs and scatters them.

In the summertime Mr. Rooster and his hens have lots to eat. They eat the grass, wild berries bugs, and even worms that they scratch out of the ground. Like Su Su's Robbins they need someone to feed them in the winter time. Mr. farmer takes them in the chicken house scatters straw and grain for them to eat. They like Mr. Farmer for feeding them and lay nice fresh eggs for his breakfast.

Dogs are more like people when it comes to eating. They get most of their food from the grocery store, out of boxes and cans. Su Su loves to watch dogs eat because they seem to enjoy it so much.

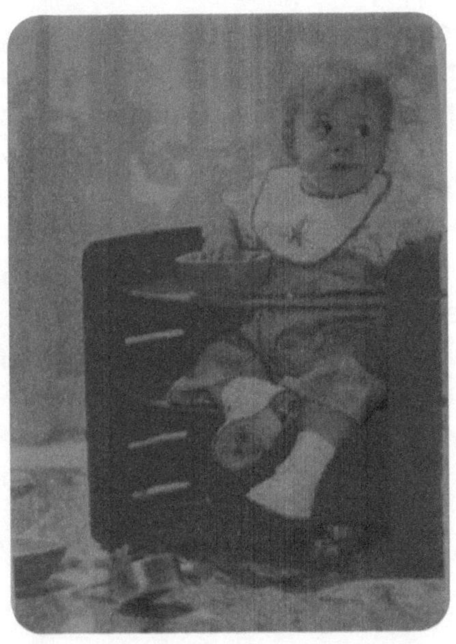

Most of all Su Su loves to watch her little brother Markie eat. He loves eating almost as much as he does his blanket. Su Su doesn't know where he puts it all but she knows it keeps him strong and healthy and about the finest little brother a girl ever had.

Sunday Eve
Jan 3 '60

Dear Susie,

We enjoyed our visit with you so very much. We got home a little after six o' clock. I know you will enjoy playing with your many nice Christmas presents.

Christmas this year has been one of the very best we have ever had. It was all because we had so many nice people here. We hope we can celebrate many more Christmases with you. You be a good girl and watch after Markie, help Mommie and Daddy, and plan to come visit us again soon.

Love and kisses,
Granbill

Dolls

Dolls are very important to all little girls and like all little girls they come in various sizes and colors. Some have blond hair like Su Su. Some have dark hair like her little

brother Markie. Some dolls have fair skins and others have dark skins. Some are girl dolls and some are boy dolls. Whether small or large, fair or dark, all dolls are dearly loved by their little mommies.

Su Su has a lot of dolls, and they are all different. She loves a paper doll named Mary. She can change her clothes in just a jiffy. One of her favorites is a beautiful lady doll with a fur coat. Su Su enjoys putting on the dolls hose and high heels. She combs her hair and dresses her in her fur coat and hats just like she was going to a party.

Su Su has another grown up doll all most as large as Su Su herself. It also has beautiful clothes. If its hair was dark it would remind Su Su of her own Mommie.

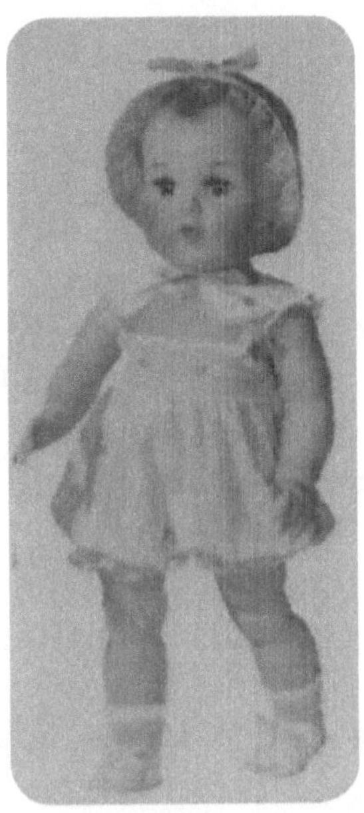

Su Su's newest doll she loves the best of all. Grannie brought it for Christmas. She loves it most because it is more like a real baby girl, not a grown up. She has several changes of clothes just for babies. Su Su dresses and cares for her dolls, so that when she is grown up and is a real mommie, she will know how to care for a real live baby.

Sunday Night
Jan 17 '60

Dear Susie,

It was nice talking to you this afternoon. I would like to be there for your birthday party. I bet you have fun. If it hadn't snowed, and Grammie was feeling better we would have come down to see you today. We have about four inches of snow already and it is still snowing.

We had a whole yard full of birds this afternoon. They were eating the bread crumbs I put out for them on the red metal table. I think maybe they flew in to see if you were here, then stayed to eat the bread.

How do you like Markie's haircut? We can hardly wait to see him. I hope you have a very happy birthday. The next one you will be a school girl won't you? It is hard for me to realize you are growing up so fast. It almost makes me want to hold back the years but I am sure we will love you just as much and be just as proud of you as you develop into a young lady.

Four Years Old

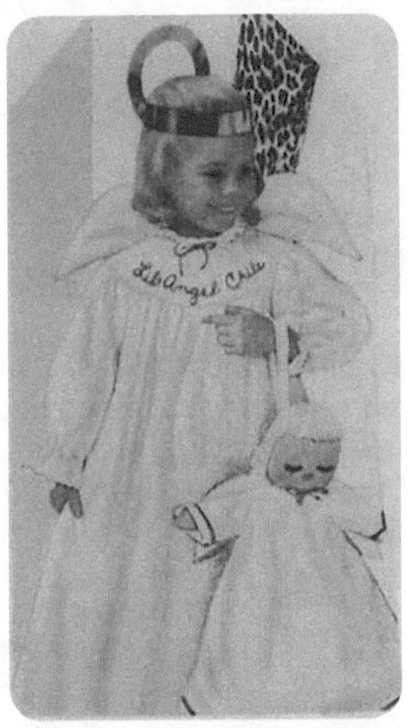

Waiting for birthdays is almost like waiting for Christmas. Su Su thinks. It is almost as exciting too. But there are presents from Mommie, Daddy, friends, Granbill and Grammie. Su Su thought her fourth birthday would never come. She would say, " Mommie when will I be four?" Mommie would say, "Just a few more days."

Finally the day arrived and Su Su was four years old! Mommie baked a birthday cake and had a party for Su Su. Her little friends came and brought presents. They had balloons and played games. Su Su blew out the candles on the cake and passed it to all her little friends.

Su Su's friends sang "Happy Birthday" as she opened her presents. She received lots of nice gifts and a cash register so she can play grocery store, some clay to mold things with, a set of dishes, a can-can petticoat and toys. Su Su thought it was the best birthday she had ever had.

Birthdays, like Christmas, come and go but Su Su doesn't mind. She is such a happy little girl. She tells her dog Chris, "There is always something nice to plan; There is Sunday School every Sunday, picnic rides into the country, trips to the park and zoo and then before long another Christmas and another birthday.

Invisible Friends

Su Su has a lot of little friends that only she can see. Some people may call them fairies or elves but Su Su knows them for real. They do many nice things for her. Su Su calls One Crispy Pink. Crispy puts the green in her lettuce, the crispness in the radishes and paints the tomatoes pink, then mixes them all together in a delicious salad for Su Su.

Sonny Straw and Susie Straw picks the finest big red ripe strawberries. They put the wonderful flavor in them, put them in a jar, cover them with sugar to make the lucious strawberry preserves that Su Su loves so well.

Sonny Straw and Susie Straw also picks the ripest, sweetest grapes just for Su Su. They squeeze the delicious juice out of them, put them in a can and freezes it. When Su Su wants grape juice all she has to do is open the can, mix the juice with some water for the most delicious drink of all.

When someone gets Su Su's goldfish bowl and splashes the water all over the floor, runs his hands in the bowl tries to catch the fish and dips some of them out flopping on the floor it isn't one of her little invisible friends, but her very much visible little brother, Markie, whom Su Su loves best of all.

Sunday Afternoon
Jan 31 '60

Dear Susie,

It was good to see and visit with you, Friday. Grammie said she was sorry she didn't get to play cards with you. She intended to but something happened and she forgot. Guess you and she will have to play that game when you come to visit us.

We liked Markie's hair cut very much. I know you must enjoy having him for a little brother. When he is a little older we would like to have both, you and he visit us. Do you suppose Mommie and Daddy could go without the both of you for a week?

I can hardly wait to get that letter you promised to write. Will you have Mommie read it to you?

Love and kisses,
Granbill

Birthdays

Birthdays are fun for everyone. When Su Su had her fourth birthday Mommie gave her a party. She had some of Su Su's very special friends there and then there was Su Su's little brother, Markie and her little cousin Timmy to help her celebrate.

Su Su loves her little brother Markie, but sometimes she can't understand how he can get into so much mischief. Of course Markie had only two birthdays himself, maybe that was why he didn't know ice cream was to eat and not dump on the floor but Su Su didn't think it was necessary for him to dump water all over the floor.

That was when Su Su's dog Chris joined the party by licking up the ice cream.

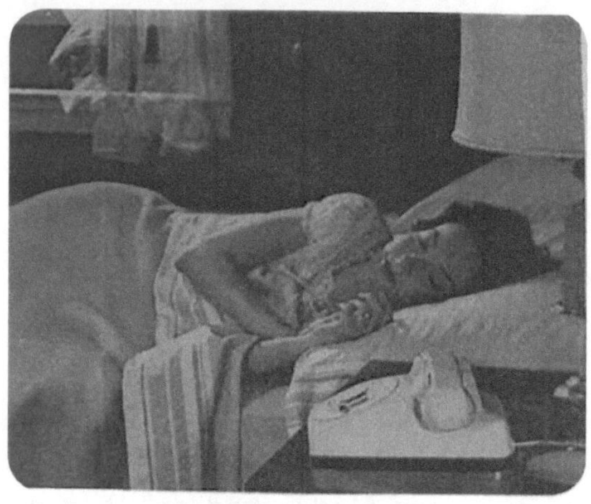

Everyone had fun at Su Su's party. When it was all over, Markie and Su Su were all tucked away for the night then Mommie could relax. As she stretched out in bed and closed her eyes she breathed a prayer of thanks that birthday comes only once a year.

Sunday Evening
Feb 7 '60

Dear Susie,

I hope next Sunday I will be visiting with you instead of writing. Grammie plans to come back to your house, from Texas. I will come down next Sunday to get her, if the weather isn't too bad. Let's hope it doesn't snow.

I was glad to get your letter. I enjoy them so much. Mommie must appreciate you cleaning up your own room. Since Grammie has been gone I could use you here to help me. I don't get much cleaning done but I get my bed made up before I go to work.

Thank Mommie for her letter. I will try to write her a little letter. I thought the picture in your story last week looked a lot like her too. It must have been taken when she was asleep since she didn't remember having it taken.

Love and kisses,
Granbill

Mommies Are Proud

One day Su Su saw a Mommie dog standing up straight with a proud look on her face. Her ears were standing straight up and her eyes wide open. Su Su had never seen a dog like that before. She asked why the dog was so happy. The mommie dog pointed toward the yard and said "That's Why."

When Su Su looked in the yard she knew why the Mommie dog was so proud. There was not one or two or three but ten beautiful, bouncing, squealing healthy puppies. They were playing with a little boy and riding in his wagon.

Next day Su Su saw a Mommie cat with the same proud happy look on her face. She was sitting up straight like the Mommie dog. Su Su knew the cat have some little baby kittens.

Sure enough sitting over by the house were five playful, soft, cuddly kittens. They were all together like they were going to have their pictures taken. As Su Su looked back at the proud mommie cat and remembered how happy the mommie dog was over her puppies, she knew they must love her kittens and puppies like her own Mommie loves she and Markie. That was why she resolved to always be kind to all little animals.

Nice People

Su Su loves books and stories. One night when she was ready to go to bed she said, "Mommie tell me a story." Mommie said " Ok Su Su, but first did you ever think how many nice people we depend on for all the many things we enjoy?" Su Su wasn't sure what Mommie was talking about, until Mommie said, "Well let's see how many we can think of."

"I know one," said Su Su "Mr. Farmer." "That is right." Said Mommie. "He plants corn and wheat that is made into cereal and breads for us to eat, he feeds the grain to chickens and cows so they can give us eggs and milk."

"I know another," said Su Su, "The grocery man. He gets the food that the farmer raises and keeps it in his store so we can buy it to eat." "That's right," said Mommie and Mommie knew Su Su wasn't just thinking of cereal, eggs, milk and bread, but also cookies, ice cream and candy.

Mommie said, "Now can you think of another? He comes to our house almost every day and once a week he has something for you," "I know," said Su Su. "The mail man." "That's right." Said Mommie. "Rain or shine he gets out in the weather delivering letters, papers, and presents, to make people happy. Now it is bedtime, Mommie said. "We will try to think of some more nice people another day." As Su Su closed her eyes to go to sleep she was thinking maybe the mailman was the nicest of all.

Sunday Night
Feb 28 '60

Dear Susie,

We still have a lot of snow here. It is getting deep out by the front walk. I fed the birds here on the red table in the backyard. I knew if you were here you would enjoy it. I hope you are staying nice and warm there. I hear you have had snow there too.

Grammie and I kept the nursery at Church tonight. We had three little girls. They were only three years old but they kept reminding me of you. It would have been nicer if you had been there too.

Did you go to Sunday School today? I think your teacher is very lucky having you in class. Write me when Mommie has time.

Love and kisses,
Granbill

Growing Up

Sometimes Su Su thinks it would be nice to be grown up. Then Mommie and Daddy wouldn't have to tell her what to eat, when to wash her face and to pick up her toys. She thinks she would like to be an actress or singer on T.V. and to have a beautiful brimed hat.

Su Su's little brother Markie is strong and active. He loves sports. He would like to be grown up and be a football star. He could play ball anytime he wanted to. In the big game he would make the winning touchdown and be a football hero.

Su Su's little cousin Timmy lives in Texas where people wear big hats and look like cowboys. Timmy can hardly wait until he grows up so he can be a real Cowboy and wear a big hat. When the horses run away with a beautiful girl he will be there to save her. She will throw her arms around his neck, give him a big kiss and say"My hero."

Su Su asked Grammie and Granbill what they would like to be since neither one was an actor or actress, nor a football star or a cowboy. She couldn't quite understand when they said they would like to have a new little red car and be young again like Su Su and Markie.

Sunday Eve
Mar 6 '60

Dear Susie,

I was so glad to get a letter from you. You write just like you talk. They are such interesting letters. Sounds like you are having lots of fun playing in the snow. Wish I could be there to watch you.

I am sorry about sending only one balloon, I could only find one. Next time I will try to get two. It was nice of you to share it with Markie.

I am proud of you for helping Mommie by making your own bed. It wont be long until Markie will be old enough to help you.

Love and Kisses,
Granbill

Mommie Remembers

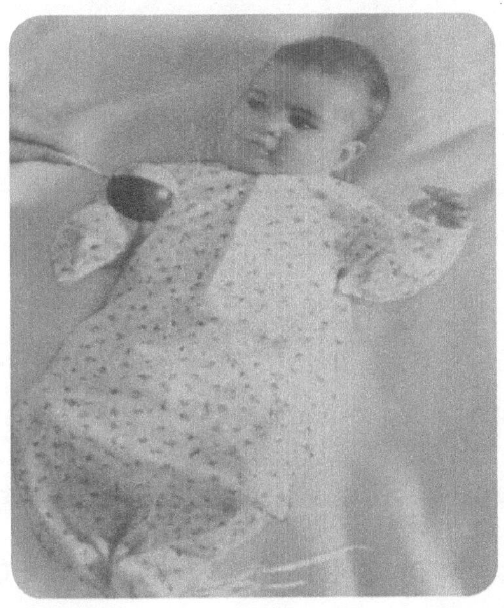

To Mommie it has been such a short time since Su Su was a little baby. Mommie thought she had never seen such a lovely little bundle of joy. Su Su was a happy baby. She gurgled and cooed at Mommie and at everyone who talked to her.

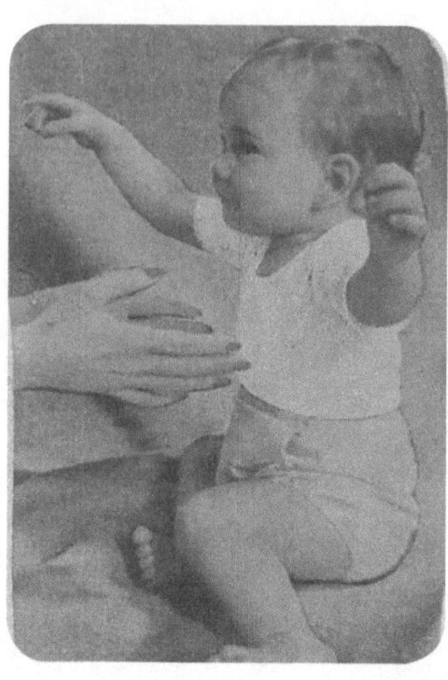

It was only a few months ago for Mommie since Su Su began to sit up and hold out her chubby little arms asking to be held. She would wave and say, "bye bye" to Daddy as he went to work. Each day she grew sweeter and dearer to Mommie, Daddy, Grammie, and Granbill.

Imagine Mommies surprise when she found Su Su making up her own bed. Now she makes it up most every day. She takes care of Markie and helps Mommie in so many different ways.

Mommie can see Su Su growing up so fast as they read books and talk together. Mommie and Daddy love Su Su even more as she is growing into a young lady. Markie loves his big sister too. In two more years Su Su will be going to school. Mommie will be a little sad as she waves to her school girl as she leaves in the morning. But Su Su will bring happiness to her.

Sunday Afternoon
Mar 20 '60

Dear Susie,

Well at last most of the snow is gone and it looks like spring may come. It is almost warm enough to work out in the yard. I think if you were here to help me I would be doing just that. I bet you are out riding around in your new car.

We should be down to see you the day after you get this letter. We can hardly wait. We won't stay long but it will be nice to see you. Maybe we can stay longer on the way back. It is now after midnight and you should be sound asleep. We have been watching TV. The late show has just gone off but I couldn't go to bed without finishing my letter to Susie.

Love and Kisses
Granbill

Sleigh Ride

Snow, snow everywhere was what Su Su saw when she looked out her window. While she had been sleeping it fell without a whisper of sound covering everything in a sparkling white blanket. Su Su could hardly wait to get her coat and boots on, then she dressed Markie, and rushed out to see how deep it was. "I just love snow, don't you Markie?" "Uh-huh." Came a muffled reply.

When Bunny rabbit woke up in his den he couldn't even see outside. Snow had covered his door, windows and roof. He loved it. He gave a sigh of relief and went back to sleep for now he wouldn't have to worry about Mr Fox catching him. He was completely hidden from all his enemies.

Snow makes most people happy. Everything is so beautiful and clean looking. Boys and girls have fun skating and ski-ing. Bunny rabbits catch up on their sleep. Su Su enjoys feeding the birds and watching them from her window. But sometimes Mommies get stuck in the snow with their cars and that isn't so funny.

Best of all, Su Su loves to go sleigh riding. As her sled speeds so fast and silently down the hill she can't help but let out a squeal of joy and she hopes the snow will stay for another day.

Sunday Night
Apr 10 '60

Dear Susie,

I wished for you today to help me paint the fence. The folks next door are putting up a picket fence. They extended mine to the front of the garage. I painted that part this afternoon.

Are you counting the days until Easter? It will only be a few more days. I bet you will be pretty all dressed up in your Easter finery. Wish I could be there to help you hunt eggs.

Love and kisses,
Granbill

New Car Travel

Su Su's Daddy brought the family a new car. It is a beautiful car all white with gold trim. Su Su is very proud of it. She and Markie are careful to clean their shoes before getting into it and not to stand on the seats. She wants to keep it nice and new looking.

It is just the finest ever to go riding in the country. There Su Su enjoys all the beautiful trees and flowers, the birds and animals. She sees the cows that give her milk, the chickens that give eggs. She sees the wheat growing in the fields from which is made bread and cereal for her breakfast.

The new car will take Su Su to the lake where she can go fishing and boat riding. Su Su loves to fish. She hopes someday she will catch a fish so big Daddy will have to help her pull it in.

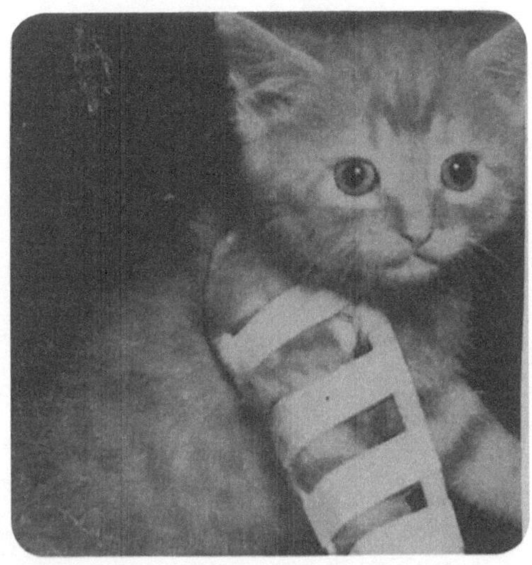

Cars are nice to have and enjoy but they can also be dangerous. Tabby cat knows that, for now he has to wear a splint on his little broken leg because he ran into the street in front of a car. That is why Su Su doesn't run into the street and always watches out for cars in her driveway.

Sunday Night
Apr 17 '60

Dear Susie,

I wonder how many Easter eggs you found today? I wish I could have been there to help you hunt.

We went to Church at eight thirty this morning and Sunday School afterwards. For dinner we had ham, green beans, salad, potatoes, hot rolls, jello and cake for dessert. Wish you could have been here. That would have made our Easter complete.

It looks like Spring is really here. It has been so nice and warm for the past few days. Everything has begun to grow and looks so pretty. When I see something pretty I am reminded of you.

Love and kisses,
Granbill

Easter

Spring is a beautiful time of the year for Su Su. She loves the nice warm days and the cool spring showers. They help to turn the whole outdoors into a beautiful garden of green grass, green leaves and colorful flowers.

Easter comes in the spring too. It is a time of gladness and joy. Su Su loves to dress up in her finest clothes and her Easter bonnet and go to Church. She and Mommie are beautiful in their Easter clothes. Markie and Daddy dress up too. Su Su doesn't know exactly whether they are beautiful or not but she thinks they are handsome and is proud of them as they all go to Church together.

After Church Su Su and Markie hunt Easter eggs. They are colored blue, red, yello and green. She and Markie make a game of seeing who can find the most eggs. Su Su found the most this year but she thinks Markie will be the winner next Easter. They had fun playing in the park and having a picnic lunch of eggs. Of course Su Su's dolls were invited to the picnic.

In the afternoon Daddy took them all for ride in their new car. They all had fun together. It was all a very happy experience for a little girl all dressed up in her Easter Bonnet.

Easter

Sunday Night
Apr 24 '60

Dear Susie,

How is my best girl? I sure miss seeing you. Wish you lived just across town so I could run over and get you for the day. Better yet just next door so I could see you every day. I mowed the lawn today and as I was mowing I was thinking of the many times you were here helping me, sure made me want to see you.

Grammie is at the Church on a committee meeting. I have the T.V. all to myself. I got to see a Western that I have never seen before because it is on the same time as the Cheyy Show. Now while, What's My Line, is on I will visit with you.

What program do you like best? I bet Markie likes Westerns. Does he still go around saying Lawman?

When are you going to come and stay a week with us?

Love and kisses,
Granbill

Saving Money

Su Su loves to go shopping with Mommie. At the grocery store they buy lots of good things to eat, sometimes even candy and ice cream. Other times they just go window shopping. They walk by the store windows and look at all the pretty things for sale. Sometimes Markie goes along and helps them look but he usually wants to look at things that are of no interest to Mommie and Su Su.

One day when Su Su saw an extra pretty dress she said, "Mommie, can I buy it?" "I'm afraid not," said Mommie. "We can't buy everything we see." Then Su Su had a bright idea. "Mommie, Granbill sends me a dime every week, if I save it and with what Daddy gives me, how long would it be before I would have enough to buy it?" "Exactly ten weeks" said Mommie, "And I think that is a wonderful idea."

Next week when Su Su got her money from Daddy and Granbill she put it in her bank. It was hard to do when all the other kids took their money and went to the candy store for ice cream and candy. When she wanted so bad to buy candy, Su Su would just think of the pretty dress and in the bank would go her money.

At last the day arrived when Su Su had enough money for her dress. Away she and Mommie headed for the store. Su Su could hardly wait she was so afraid it would be gone but it was still there and was a perfect fit. It was such a beautiful dress and Su Su was so happy. When the other kids saw her in it, and how pretty she was they wished they had saved their money too.

Sunday Afternoon
May 1 '60

Dear Susie,

I didn't receive your letter last week that Mommie said you were sending. What happened, did she forget to put it in her letter? I can hardly wait to get it. We hope you will bring Mommie and Markie and stay a week with us. Of course we would be glad to have Daddy too but we know he will have to work.

We are sending you two new dresses, Grammie found for you yesterday. We hope you like them because we enjoy getting them for you. Tell Markie we haven't forgotten him and will do something for him next. Grammie is so pleased that he remembers her.

Love and Kisses
Granbill

Dreamland

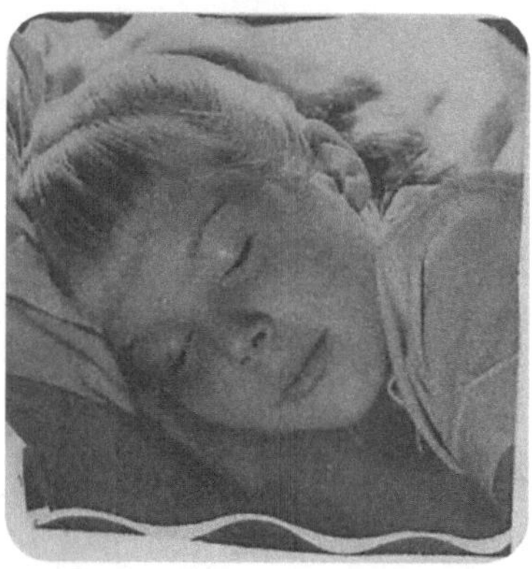

Dreamland is one of Su Su's favorite places. After a busy day playing she loves to take a bath and put on her pretty pajamas then into a nice clean bed. In a few minutes she is off to dreamland and new adventures. She never knows exactly where her dreams will take her or whom she may be.

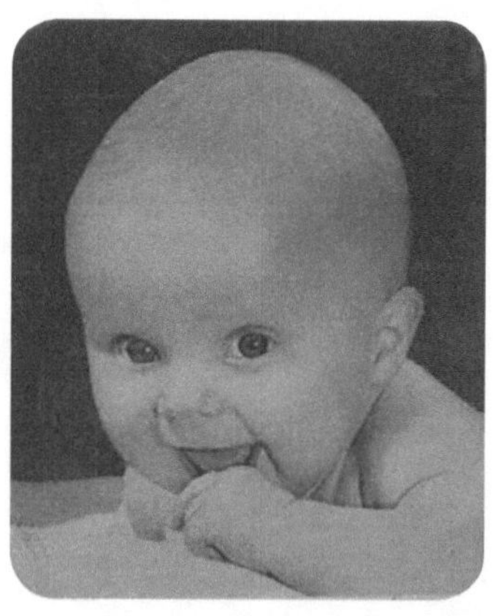

Once she dreamed she was a little baby again with a slick bald head instead of her pony tail. It was fun being a little baby but being grown up too. She could understand what everyone was saying when they "cooed" and talked baby talk. She could hardly keep a straight face when people made funny ones trying to make her laugh.

Another time she had a grocery store and sold good things to eat for people that came to her store. She liked owning a grocery because she had lots of candy and ice cream. The dream was so real one time she even woke up with a tummy ache.

Another time she was the zoo keeper at the park. There she played with and fed all the animals. She had to be careful around the bears and lions. The monkeys were a barrel of fun. She loved the deer. They would come and eat from her hand. Their horns reminded Su Su of a hat rack.

Dreamland is a nice experience for Su Su but never quite as thrilling as waking up to a bright new day.

Dreamland

Sunday Night
May 8 1960

Dear Susie,

Well your letter finally came and it was worth waiting
for. It was almost like a visit with you. I am glad you
liked your storey. Sometimes I wonder if you haven't
outgrown them. I love to do them for you as long as you
enjoy them but when the time comes that they are of no
interest to you, let me know and I will discontinue them.

If I can get all my work caught up in the next few days,
we will be down to see you later part of this week.
Maybe you, Mommie and Markie can come home
with us.

I am happy that you like your Sunday School for I think
it is very important that you go. It would be nicer for me
if you lived here and we could go together.

This is Mother's Day. What did you get Mommie for
her present? I am glad you have such a nice Mommie.

Aren't you?

Love and Kisses,
Granbill

Like Mommie

One day when Su Su was with Mommie she began to wonder what she would do when she grew up. "What should I do when I grow up Mommie" She asked. "There are lots of nice things you could do" said Mommie. "What would you like to do most?" "I don't know." Replied Su Su.

"I will suggest some things, and see if there are any of them you would like to do." Suggested Mommie. "You could be a musician, and play music for people to enjoy. You could play for Sunday school and Church. You could play for people when they come to visit you. You would have to do a lot of practicing and studying." "What else could I do?" Asked Su Su.

"You could be a nurse and care for people who are sick. You could work in a hospital or you could visit people in their homes." Said Mommie. "Nurses are needed and do a wonderful work." Su Su thought it would be nice to be a nurse but wasn't for sure if it was something she wanted to do.

When Su Su looked at her Mommie and thought what a wonderful person she was, she had an idea. "Why couldn't I just be a Mommie?" She asked. "Then I could stay home and care for my children and cook for my husband." "That is a wonderful thing to do too," said Mommie. "Then that's what I will do," said Su Su. "And I think I will tell Markie, he should be a Mommie too."

Christmas

To Su Su and Granbill it seemed like Christmas would never come.

At last the day came. Daddy loaded the car with Mommie, Su Su, and Markie along with a lot of presents. They were off to Grammie's and Grandbill's house. Christmas Eve Su Su went to Church with Grammie and Granbill.

The whole room was full of presents. A garage and farm set for Markie and guns for both along with a lot of other things. A doll, a bathinett and a doll buggy for Su Su. Daddy, Mommie, Pat, Grammie, Granbill got just the presents they had wanted. It was a joyous and happy time for all.

Christmas was a birthday party too. Su Su knew she was celebrating the Birthday of Jesus, born in a manger many, many years ago and it was He who brought to the world, the hope, joy and happiness of Christmas.

Sat Night
Dec 31 1960

Dear Susie,

Christmas this year has come and gone but the memories of it will be with us for a long time. It was one of the happiest for Grammie and me. Having all the family together made it complete.

It is kinda quite around here tonight. We could use you to keep us company. We hope you can come for a week or so real soon. Are you and Markie having fun playing with your Christmas presents? It is only thirty minutes until this year will be gone and the new one will be here. We hope it will be a most happy one for you, Markie, Mommie and Daddy.

Love and Kisses,
Granbill

Vacation

Su Su loves vacations. It is one of the best times of the year for her. One of the things she enjoys most is having Mommie, Daddy, and Markie with her. They get in the car and drive all day. They see the farms with lots of animals, the beautiful rivers, mountains and trees. They sing and play games as they drive along.

At the end of the day and several hundred miles along the way they find a motel and something to eat. While Mommie enjoys a nice hot bath in the tub, Su Su, Markie, and Daddy head for the swimming pool. Su Su loves the pool. With water wings she floats around and when she kicks and pulls with her arms she can swim like Daddy.

Another day on the road over mountains and through the deserts they were in California. There they visited a lot of relatives Su Su had never seen before. It didn't take her long to get acquainted. She loved them and they loved her. Su Su also found that oranges grew on trees instead of the grocery counters.

One of the things Su Su, will remember a long time is visiting Disney land. It was almost like the fairy lands she had read about only with rides. Another thrilling experience was swimming in the ocean. It was the most water Su Su had ever seen. The waves were higher than her head. When they were coming in Su Su had to run towards the shore to keep them from covering her. Now that Christmas has passed and a New Year is starting, Su Su is again looking forward to another vacation.

Sun Night
Jan 15 '61

Dear Susie,

I just finished watching the Roy Rogers show, Marine Land, hoping they snapped a shot of you. Guess the cameras were not focused at the right place since I didn't see your smiling face.

Only three more days until you will be five years old. I wish I could be there to help you celebrate your birthday. It seems such a short time go ago since you were a little baby.

It has been a joy to see you grow from a tiny baby to such a fine pretty five year old girl. I know Mommie and Daddy must be very proud of you.

We are still having beautiful weather here. Hardly seems like winter time. It makes me want to get outside and start planting a garden or better yet go fishing. Maybe in a few weeks we can come down and you can go fishing with me.

Love and Kisses,
Granbill

Su Su in Drawings

It made Mommie want to spank but with that impish smile, all she could do was smile back.

"What did I do at two?" Asked Su Su. "Let me think" said Mommie. "Your table manners had improved but you had found ways to keep from going to sleep. At bed time it was, "Mommie I want a drink, Mommie I want my doll" and Mommie I want to go to the baths rooms." These were the times when Mommie could hardly wait for you to grow up."

"At three," Mommie said, "You were learning to do lots of things. You could help take care of Markie, Pick up toys, clean up your room and answer the telephone. You loved to read and color and carry on a conversation like a grown up. You went to Grammie's and Granbill's house and stayed a week or so with them."

"Tell me about four," Said Su Su. "Let's see some of the things you are learning to do now." Mused Mommie. "First you learned to dress up like Mommie in her shoes and hat. You can wash and dry dishes. You keep your room straight and talk like a lady. Do you know that Wednesday you will be five and will soon be a school girl? "Oh Mommie I just love birthdays," Cried Su Su. "And each year brings something new and interesting. Maybe I don't want to grow for another few years," Concluded Su Su.

Sunday Night
Jan 22 '61

Dear Susie,

It was very nice of you to call me as part of your birthday present. That way I got a present too. I guess I will have to try that on my own birthday to repay you. It was too bad Markie had chicken-pox and that you couldn't go to the show. Hope Markie is getting well. It's no fun to be sick.

I can hardly wait to see your new bicycle. That is a real fine present. You be careful about cars when you are riding. Grammie and I thought it would be nice to bring it up here when you come to visit us. You would have a lot of sidewalk and drive way to ride it on.

We thought the pictures of you and Markie with the bicycle were very good. They made us want to see you. You have grown a lot since you lived with us in Wichita. That cute little blond with the curly hair and the eyes that laughed has grown into quite a little lady.

Love and Kisses,
Granbill

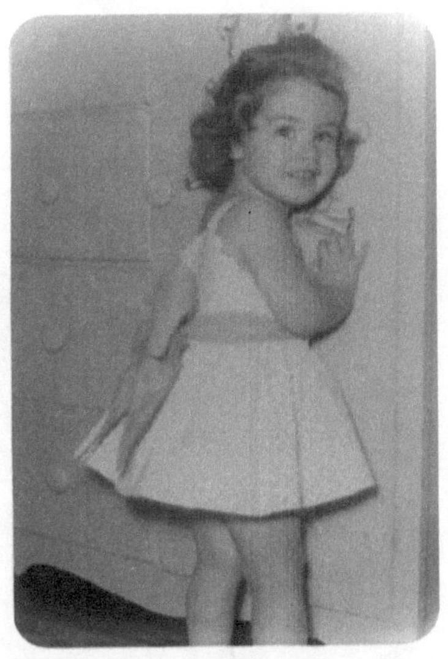

At last the day arrived when everything worked out. Grammie and Granbill drove down to get Su Su. She still had her bag packed and ready to go. It was hard to tell who was the happiest, Su Su or Granbill. As they drove along to Wichita, Granbill was thinking how she had grown since she moved from Wichita over two years ago.

Snow!

Most times snows are nice to have. Su Su loves to ride on the snow in a sled and go zooming along. She sometimes makes snow balls to throw. If she hits Markie with them it doesn't hurt because they are light and soft. If she falls off her sled, in the snow, it doesn't bother her. It's just like soft sand only colder.

Snows are also beautiful. They make everything so white and clean. Snows paint wonderful pictures out of trees and shrubs. The soft glittering whiteness on lacely branches is more beautiful than flowers and leaves that cover the same branches in the spring.

Snows are helpful bringing moisture to the trees and shrubs so they will put on leaves and flowers in the spring. Snow helps to cause the grains to come up and make wheat and food for Su Su to eat. It helps keep the streams full of pure water so the fish will grow and bite at Su Su's hook when she goes fishing with Daddy.

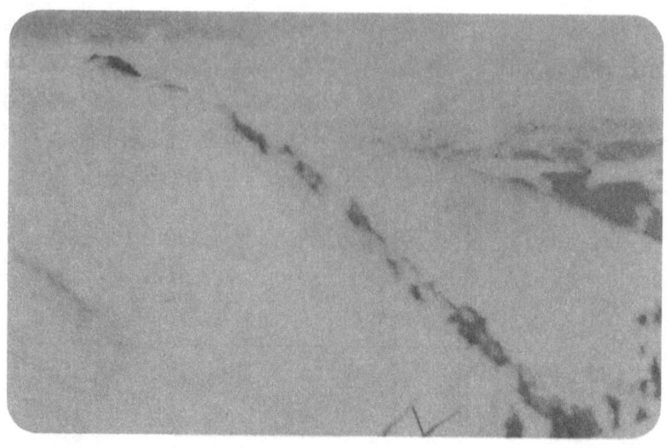

Most times, Granbill loves snow. All week long he had been looking forward to going to see Su Su and bringing her home with him. Grammie and he shopped for groceries that Su Su would like, Cheries, extra milk, and candy bars.

They got up early Sunday Morning to go to Su Su's but when they looked out everything was covered with snow. They knew it would be too slick to drive on. That meant it would be another week before they could have Su Su. That was one time Granbill didn't like the snow.

Snow!

Monday Morning
Feb 20 1961

Dear Susie,

You are probably home by now and we have just finished breakfast. It will soon be time for me to get ready to go to work. I just wanted to write you a short note and tell you how much we enjoyed having you with us for the past week. We hope you enjoyed it as much as we did. Maybe we can have you again before long. I didn't have time to get the blue balloons to send this time but will see if I can find some next time.

I know Mommie, Daddy, and Markie are glad to have you home. You will be a big help to Mommie, I am sure.

Love and Kisses,
Granbill

Little To Big

Su Su like all five year old girls loves to play. She loves to read to relax and to eat, but like a lot of other little people, she sometimes does big important things.

Su Su helps Mommie around the house. She does things like washing the dishes and helping cook. She also does really important, grown up things, helping Mommie buy groceries, selecting the kind of foods that keeps all of her family happy and healthy.

Su Su little brother Markie, sometimes makes extra work for Mommie and Su Su, leaving his toys for them to pick up and spilling things while trying to help Mommie.

Sunday Night
March 5 1961

Dear Susie,

I loved the letter you wrote me this week. It was very interesting and well written. Mommies letter was nice too. Did you help her write it? There is hardly a day goes by that Grammie and I don't remember and talk about the fun we had when you visited us. We hope you enjoyed it too and have many pleasant memories of the times you have brought so much sunshine to our lives.

Love and kisses,
Granbill

At Granbill's

Su Su and Granbill had lots of fun when she visited him. They colored pictures in Su Su's color book. Granbill couldn't stay in the lines as well as she did. They played games with picture cards and Su Su won most of the games but Granbill didn't mind. He always knew Su Su was a very smart grandaughter. He can't decide whether she is as smart as she is pretty or as pretty as she is smart.

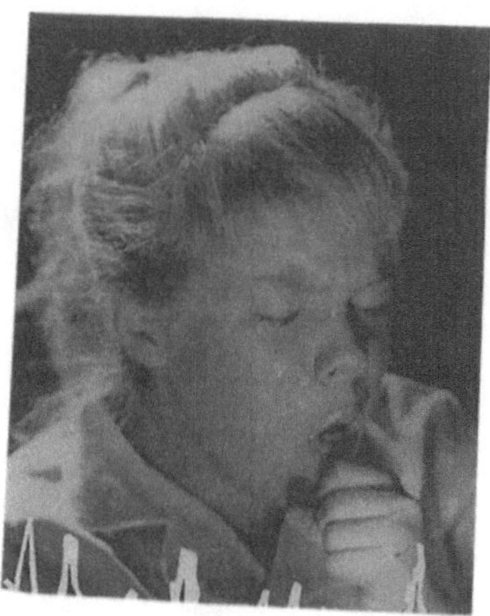

One night Su Su had a cold and coughed but Grannie knew just what to do. She greased Su Su's throat with Vicks salve and covered it with a warm cloth. In a few minutes Su Su was back to dreamland.

Su Su went shopping with Granbill at the grocery store, Su Su helped push the cart and put groceries in the basket. They got lots of good things to eat. The thing Su Su liked best was when they went by the candy counter. "Sweets for the Sweet." said Granbill and it would take a lot of candy to be as sweet as Su Su.

At Granbill's

Sunday Night
Mar 12 '61

Dear Susie,

Next Sunday we plan to spend with you. Hope it is a bright and sunny day. It is cloudy and raining a little here today, of course we need a little rain along with the sunshine. Just like we need some work and a lot of play, or had you rather play all the time? Maybe you should work a little, like picking up your clothes and toys, helping mommie with Markie and the dishes. You will be learning to do the things now that will be of value to you when are grown up and are a mommie yourself. I sometimes wonder how mommies can get so many things done- don't you?

Be seeing you soon.

Love and kisses,
Granbill

Mommies know

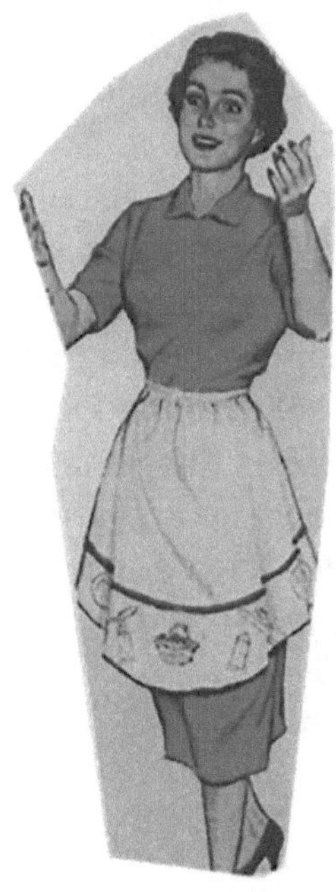

Mommies have to answer a lot of questions. Asking the questions are, Daddy, Markie, and Su Su. As Mommie answers the queries, Su Su sometimes wonders how any one could learn so much.

Daddy asks questions like, Where are my socks? Do I have a shirt ironed ready to wear? Where is My pipe? Where are the car keys? Where is my tie pin? Where is my pencil? What are we having for dinner?

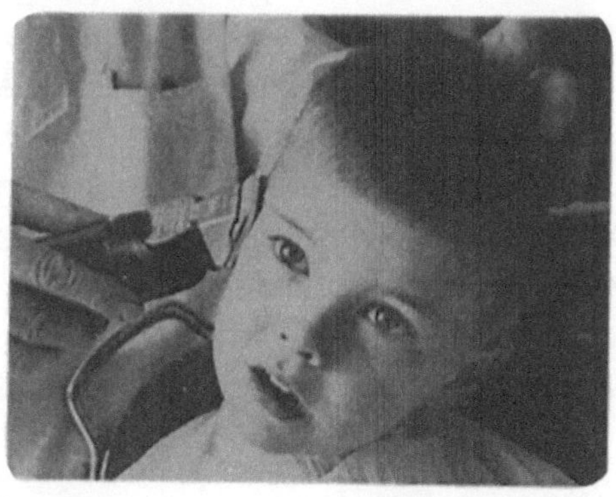

Su Su wonders where Markie gets all the questions he asks. Where does dust come from? Where can he find his blanket and some lint to tickle his nose? Where does the sun go when it gets dark? Where are the stars in the day time? Why is it cold in the winter and warm in the summer? Why doesn't it hurt when the barber cuts his hair?

What Markie doesn't think to ask Su Su does. Where am I when I am asleep? Does my dog Chrisie Dream? How can Santa ride his sleigh when there is no snow? Some questions Mommie has trouble answering, but the ones Su Su asks about keeping house and homemaking, Mommie can answer easy. It is these questions that helps Su Su to learn the things she needs to know when she is a mommie herself.

Mommies know

Sunday Night
Mar 25 Easter

Dear Susie,

Next Sunday is Easter. We are wondering if you will be coming to spend it with us. We would be happy to have you but we will understand if you can't make it. I bet you will be pretty in your Easter outfit.

It has been raining here most all day. The grass is getting green the trees are budding out and it will soon be spring. I know you are looking forward to the fun that comes with the warm days of Spring.

Give our love to your Mommie, Daddy and Markie and keep a lot for yourself.

Love and kisses,
Granbill

Spring

Spring is a happy time at Su Su's house. The flowers begin to bloom. The grass turns from brown to green. The trees put on their leaves. The birds begin to build their nests, and Mommies start their Spring house cleaning.

Su Su's Daddy begins to think of fishing. Playing golf in the sunshine and if it gets too warm to work or play, swimming will be fun.

Markie gets out his guns, his cowboy outfits and is ready to hit the dusty trail in the back yard or park. He has fun rounding up bugs, ants, frogs or anything else that runs or crawls.

Su Su can hardly wait to get outside where she can play house and have picnics or ride her bicycle. She loves the beautiful flowers and the songs of her little bird friends. Next to Christmas time, Su Su thinks spring is one of the happiest times of the year.

Spring

Sunday Night
Apr 9 '61 Bird House

Dear Susie,

I hear a bird out front singing, just now, like he was ready to go house hunting. You may have seen the bird house, I made this winter. I painted it red and hung it in the tree at the back of our yard but so far I haven't seen any birds looking it over. Could be I got it too red, anyway it looks pretty hanging out there. I would bet some bird will take possession before Spring has passed.

Wish I could have gone along fishing with you last week. Its too bad you didn't have better luck but it sounded like fun.

Tell Markie we want him to come some time too and stay a week.

Love and kisses,
Granbill

Sunday Night
Apr 16 '61 Bird House

Dear Susie,

Guess what? I looked out the window this week to the tree where I hung the bird house and it wasn't there. The wind had blown it down. Luckily the birds hadn't moved in yet. It landed right side up so it didn't hurt the house. I will have to use heavier wire when I put it up again tomorrow.

We will have to visit the zoo again when you come to see me.

Love and kisses,
Granbill

Sunday Night
Apr 23 '61 Bird House

Dear Susie,

Here it is Sunday night again. I wonder if the weeks go by as fast for you, or is it, that as we grow older the time goes by faster? I don't mind for the days to go so fast because I get to visit you that much sooner every Sunday by letter.

Well Spring has really arrived here. I just can't understand though, why some birds don't move into the house I made for them. So far it is empty. I guess I will have to put up a sign saying it ready for them to move in.

I mowed the yard this afternoon. I always remember how you helped me with it when you were here, also the time you found the rock and threw it into the air and then caught it on the top of your head. I saw the nurse last week that helped with the stitches, when they sewed up the cut, the rock made. She remembered you.

Give my love to Mommie, Daddy, and Markie and keep a lot for yourself.

Love and kisses,
Granbill

Sunday Eve.
Apr 30 '61 Bird House

Dear Susie,

I'm still having bird house trouble. None have moved in yet. Oh well, we can always use it for a target to throw rocks at.

Next week I will get to talk to you instead of writing. I can hardly wait. Hope you are looking forward to it also.

Love and kisses,
Granbill

Bird House

Su Su's Granbill built a bird house. He painted it red and hung it up in a tree. He waited and waited for some birds to move in. He was sure some happy birds, house hunting, would move right in but he was be disappointed.

First came some Red birds to inspect it. They looked it over very carefully. They chirpped and hopped around. They even brought some berries and hung them on a limb close by the house. Granbill couldn't understand why they didn't move in unless the red on the house clashed with the red on their feathers but they decided against moving in.

The Blue Jays came next. They seemed very interested. Mr Jay flew to a limb close to the house, cocked his head first one way then the other, looking it over. He nodded his head up and down in approval but Mrs Jay shook hers No. Since she would spend more time in it, Mr Jay agreed with her. They flew away.

Some sparrows came next. Granbill was sure they would move in because they are not too particular about their house. They don't even make a neat nest and are very messy housekeepers. That is why most people don't want them around but Granbill was getting desperate. When he discovered that they had built a nest outside on a limb and even hatched their babies, it was too much! Right then and there he took the house down and decided to let the birds build their own houses!

Rain

"Mommie what makes it rain?" asked Su Su, " Well lets see." said Mommie. " It takes the ocean, lakes,streams, the sun and gravity." Su Su knew what the sun, lakes, streams, and the ocean was but she was puzzled about gravity, she asked," Mommie, what is gravity?, " It's what makes a ball come down when it is tossed into the air." Mommie explained.

"How does the sun help it rain when it is usually behind a cloud when it rains?" asked Su Su. The sun warms the water in the lakes, streams, and oceans causing it to evaporate like steam from a kettle of water boiling." replied Mommie, "then it rises into the air and makes clouds.

" When the clouds become too heavy to float," continued Mommie. "Gravity pulls it down again in the form of rain; snow, sleet, or hail. The snow, hail and sleet melts after it falls and like rain some sinks into the ground and the rest runs back into the lakes, streams and oceans."

"Rain makes flowers and things grow," said Su Su. "That's right," replied Mommie. "It also makes grain, fruits, and vegetables grow for you to eat," said Mommie. "If I didn't have something to eat I wouldn't grow," Su Su reasoned. "Gee! I am glad for oceans, rivers, lakes, sun, and gravity," said Su Su.

Eating Is Fun

Su Su loves to eat. She loves good food and food that is good for her. Su Su's Granbill loves to eat and he likes to cook too. Sometimes Grammie wonders if he wouldn't rather cook than to eat.

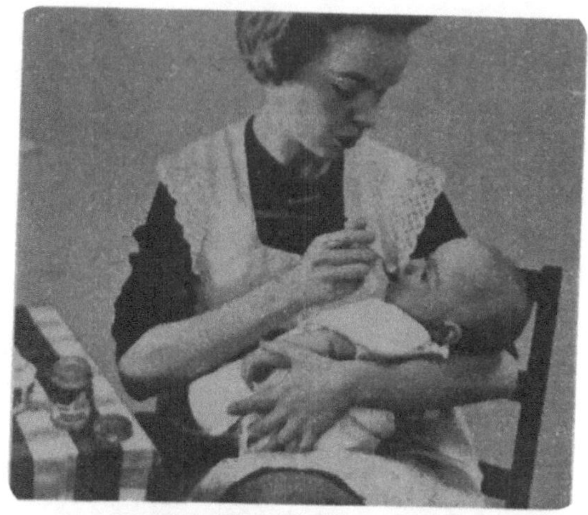

Su Su is a very dainty eater. She takes small bites and chews her food well. She is polite and says please when asking for food and thank You when she receives it. Her table manners are very good. Su Su eats vegetables, fruits, bread, meat, and other foods that help her to grow. Like a lot of little girls she has a sweet tooth too for ice cream and cake.

Markie, Su Su's little brother loves to eat too. He is polite but he isn't dainty. His favorite food is meat and he doesn't have to ask for it to be passed. He manages very well for himself when Mommie's back is turned.

Sunday Afternoon
May 27 1961

Dear Susie,

Well, it seems like summer is here at last. The sun has been bright all day and it's warm. We took our chairs out in the back yard and took a sun bath. It sure felt good after so much cool weather.

Would you like to have a little sister or brother? It would be cute if it looked like either you or Markie.

Love and kisses,
Granbill

Sunday Night
June 4 '61

Dear Susie,

We are getting anxious to see you. It will be nice if you can come to see us next week end. Hope it works out so you can, if you don't I guess we will have to come see you before long. We are glad you will be getting your new house soon. We will sure have to come down just as soon as you get moved in.

Love and kisses,
Granbill

Dentist

One day Mommie said, "Su Su you are getting old enough that we should have your teeth checked." Su Su was puzzled. "I don't need checked, Mommie, they are still in my mouth." She replied. "I didn't mean checked to see if you still have them," Laughed Mommie. "I meant, to see if they need filling."

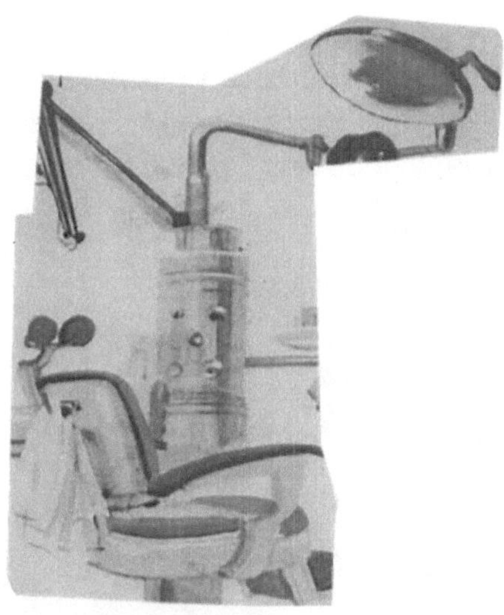

The dentist was very friendly and Su Su liked him immediately. She climbed up into a big soft chair that leaned back and could be moved up and down. "Open wide," Said the dentist. Su Su opened her mouth wide and he looked inside with a tiny mirror. "Everything looks fine." He said, "but come back in six months for another check."

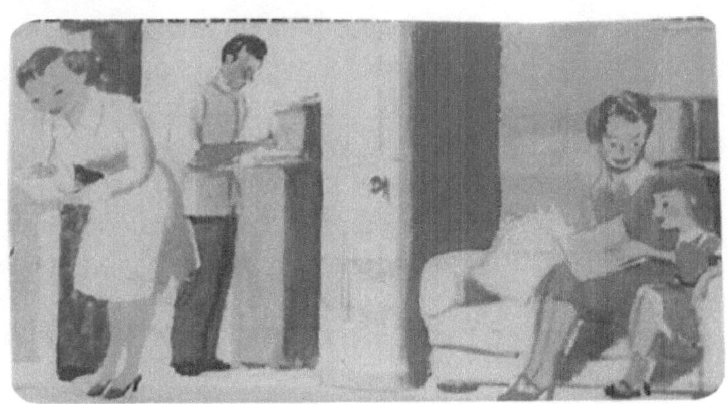

Mommie took Su Su back in six months. This time they had to wait until the nurse and dentist were through with another patient. Su Su didn't mind because there was lots of magazines and books to look at while they waited.

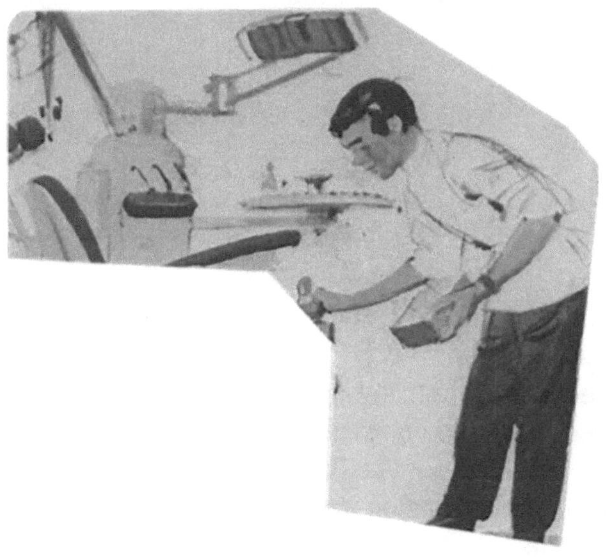

When the dentist examined Su Su's teeth this time he found a small cavity. He put a small buzzer into her mouth. It was a drill. He said it might hurt a little and it did, about like a bee sting. "You are a brave girl but now that I have filled that cavity everything is swell again and your teeth are good and strong. He gave Su Su some candy for being a brave girl . Now she doesn't mind having her teeth checked but she brushes them every day.

Dentist

Sunday Night
June 11 '61

Dear Susie,

I wonder if you will be in your new home by the time
I write you next week. You will have to send me your
new address if you are so I will know where to mail
your letter. I bet you can hardly wait to get moved in. It
is such a nice house and I am sure you will be happy
to have a room all your own.

It is now Monday morning. I must get this ready to mail
before time to go to work.

Love and kisses,
Granbill

Summer Fun

Summer time is fun time for Su Su. It is time to go to the parks and Zoos. She and Markie love to watch and feed the animals and birds.

When they get through seeing and feeding the animals, nothing is more fun than getting an ice cream cone and riding the merry-go round.

There is always a place to play in the sand and make mud pies but mud pies are no fun to eat.

When it is time to eat, there is nothing quite so good as a picnic lunch in the park with Mommie, Daddy and Markie. The sandwiches, pie, cakes, and pop taste better than at any other place or time. Summer time is fun time and Su Su loves every minute of it.

Sunday Night
June 18 '61

Dear Susie,

So you have moved into your new home. I hope the postman can find you. When he sees your letter he will be wanting to take it to 2229 ½ North West 32nd St. since he has delivered so many of them there. I am glad you sent your new address because I wouldn't have remembered it but I bet we can find it when we come down to see you next Sunday. We can hardly wait to see you in your new home. I can have a cup of hot coffee while you are eating your breakfast. Grammie is working real hard on your new drapes so we can bring them along too.

Love and kisses,
Granbill

Su Su Moves Into Her New Home

For weeks Su Su, Mommie, Daddy, and Markie had watched their new house being built. They could hardly wait for it to be finished. At last the day arrived and it was ready to move into. Next came the packing and moving. Su Su thought they would never get everything packed and into the truck, but they did, and they were on their way.

As Mommie opened the door to the new house she thought she could never be happier than she was at that moment. It was a dream come true.

Markie thought he was the happiest because now he could have a room all his own. It made him feel almost as big as Su Su.

Su Su could hardly wait to get into her own room and fix it up just the way she wanted it. Everyone, including Daddy, were so glad to be in their new home at last but each knew that the happiness they felt wasn't just the new house. It was being together and having each other.

Sunday Night
July 23, 1961

Dear Susie,

These days sure go by in a hurry. Seems only yesterday since I sent your last letter. Maybe it is because we keep so busy. Mommie says you are busy too playing with your new friends. Why don;t you write me a letter telling me their names and all about them.

I wish you could have been here to help us pick peaches tomorrow morning. They are ripe and we want to get some for the freezer.

Love and kisses,
Granbill

Farmer's Daughter

Su Su is a city girl. She lives with her Mommie, Daddy, and Brother Markie in a new home in a big city but she lives close enough to the country that she loves it too. Sometimes Mommie and Daddy read books to her and Markie about farms and animals but the only animal they have is their dog Chris.

Su Su has a big imagination that she uses to play make believe. She makes believe that Markie is farmer Brown with his straw hat, overalls, pitch fork and a cob pipe, while she is the farmer's wife, in her apron and colorful dress. It is she who raises the chickens, while Markie is out in the fields plowing corn and other vegetables.

Her chickens are make believe too. They are white with big red combs. They scratch the grass and ground to find their food. The rooster gives out with a loud cock-a-doodle-de-do crow as he sits perched on a fence post. Chris's house serves as the chicken house where they roost at night and lay their eggs.

The thing Su Su likes the best about playing farm is when Mommie helps out too. It isn't make believe when Mommie serves golden brown fried chicken, with delicious fresh vegetables. Even though it is all grown in the country, a city girl like Su Su, enjoys the food just like a farmers daughter.

Sunday Eve
Aug 6 '61

Dear Susie,

As you can see i got the typewriter fixed but I didn't get my fingers fixed so they always hit the right keys but with the help of an eraser maybe you can read this letter. If you can't why don't you let Mommie try it.

I am sure you would be a lot of help if you were here. It is too bad that you are not just around the corner and could run in any time of the day.

We are getting anxious to see you.

Granbill

Working Together

When Su Su, Mommie, Daddy, and Markie moved into their new house it also had a new yard. Su Su learned that new yards don't have pretty grass and that it takes a lot of work to make a beautiful lawn all covered with green grass and colorful flowers.

Everyone worked together at Su Su's to get the grass planted. First Daddy plowed up the ground and raked it level then he made rows for the grass to be planted in. Markie got his wagon and filled it with the green grass. As he pulled it along Su Su would drop small pieces in the places prepared by Daddy.

Mommie came along and covered the grass with fine soil so it would take root and grow. It was hot and tiresome work for everyone but they were all happy working together. Sometimes Markie, and Su Su would play a little in between working but they were a lot of help and made the planting go faster.

After every bit of the ground was watered down they went into the house to clean up. They all took cool baths that refreshed them. As they rested and relaxed they talked about how nice it would be when the grass covered all the yard like a green carpet, then they could have a picnic in their own backyard.

Sunday Eve
Aug 13 '61

Dear Susie,

It was nice to get your letter and to hear all about your new friends. I am glad Markie has a new friend too. Sounds like they would be a lot of fun. I bet you are getting excited about school, it won't be long now will it?

Mommie will be taking a big step when she sees you off to school for the first time. It will be hard on her to see her little girl leave the first morning but she will just have to grow up like you won't she?

I bet Markie misses you the most. He will be watching every afternoon for the school bus that brings her sister home.

I just know you will be a good student and will learn fast. First thing you know, you will be writing me without the help of Mommie and you will be reading stories to Markie from your school books.

It has been cool and rainy all day here. We went to Sunday School and Church this morning and have just been lazy the rest of the time.

Give my love to Mommie, Daddy, and Markie, and keep a lot for yourself.

Love and kisses,
Granbill

Vacation

Su Su likes to swim. She enjoys the cool water as she splashes around. When she went on vacation last year she saw the ocean for the first time. She had never seen so much water before. As far as she could see there was nothing but blue rolling water. With sand buckets she and Markie raced along the beach. The sun was shining bright but it was cool as the wind blew in from the water.

There was so much to find and explore, beautiful sea shells that used to house tiny ocean creatures. They were all shapes and sizes, the colors were never ending. It was so much fun to sit on the sand and hunt for them. The ocean brought in a new supply as it came rolling in. There were rocks and pebbles in almost as many colors as the sea shells.

Sometimes the ocean would come in so far Su Su and Markie would have to grab their sand buckets and race up the beach to keep the water from covering them. They ran to where their Daddy was sunning himself. He was almost asleep as he lay on the sand. He came awake with a start as they dumped cold water on him.

Another race was on as he jumped up to chase them. They headed back to the water with Daddy right behind them. It all ended up happily when he caught up with them and the ocean at the same time. As a big wave hit them they all fell down with a loud splash and a hearty laugh. Seeing and playing in the ocean and on the beach was one of the highlights of Su Su's vacation.

Sunday Night
Aug 20 '61

Dear Susie,

We enjoyed Mommies letter. Sounds like you are getting all ready for school. Are you getting excited about it? I am.

Love and kisses,
Granbill

New Friends

Su Su loves all her friends but she also has learned to play alone. When her little friends are not around she can entertain herself playing with her dolls.

One of the nicest things about moving to her new house was finding and making new friends. The one she likes the best is Pam who lives just across the street. She is only one year older than Su Su and they have fun playing together.

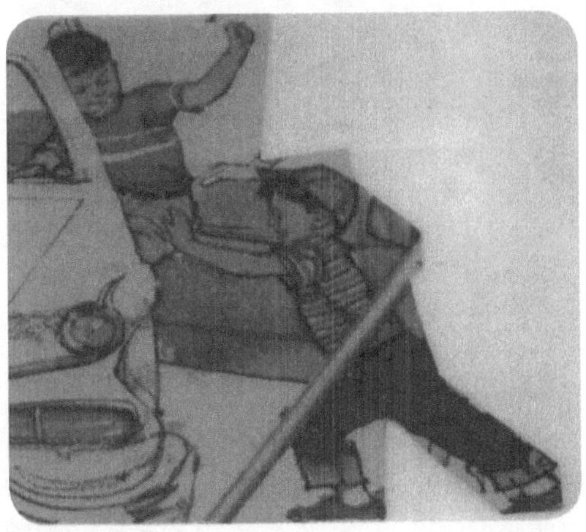

Markie found a new friend too. He is Pam's little brother, jimmy, and he is just a year older than Markie. A year doesn't make much difference when you are three and four years old. Markie and Jimmy have just as much fun playing together as their big sisters do.

In just another week or so, Su Su and Pam will be going off to school together. There they will find a lot of new friends and adventures. Even though they will enjoy all their new friends, it is nice to have an extra special friends who lives just across the street.

Sunday Night
Sept 3 '61

Dear Susie,

I will try to address your letter right this time. I am sorry the one I sent you last week was late. By the time you get this you will be a school girl. I hope you have a real nice teacher. You will have to write and tell me all about her, also about the school bus and where it picks you up.

Write me a letter when Mommie has time.

Love and kisses,
Granbill
Sunday Night
Sept 10, 1961

Dear Susie,

I know this has been a busy week for you. How do you like being a school girl? We were glad to know the bus will come close to your house. It will be nice when it rains or snows to have them pick you up so close to home.

In another week we will be starting our vacation. It seems a little strange going on vacation this time of year when most people have returned from theirs, and with school and all the fall activities starting. It will be nice though to visit you again so soon.

I can hardly wait to see your school books and to get a report on how you like being a school girl.

Love and kisses,
Granbill

Starts to School

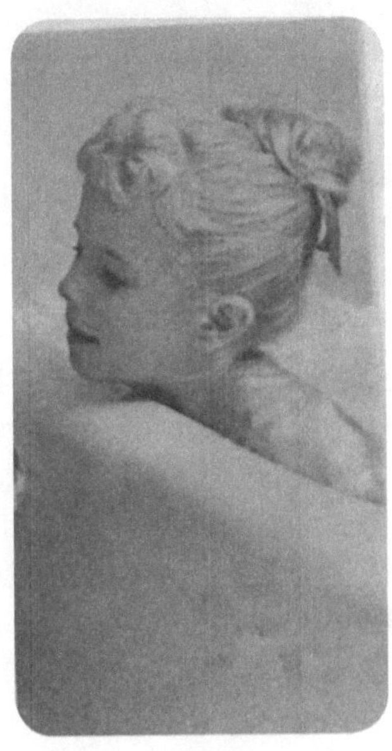

It had been a long time, to Su Su, from her babyhood to a big five year old school girl. When Mommie said, "Su Su will soon be in school." It seemed ages until the day arrived, but the day finally came, and Su Su had never been so scrubbed and combed. It was important to be well groomed the first day at school.

Su Su didn't sleep very well the night before, for just thinking about her big adventure in the morning. When the day dawned Su Su was up bright and early. Mommie didn't have time to be very sad seeing her little girl off to school for the first time, she was too busy getting Su Su ready and Daddy off to work at the same time. Su Su's brother Markie, was a little sad as he watched his big sis skip off on her way to school.

It was exciting meeting her teacher and getting her books assigned and a desk all her own. Like all boys and girls, Su Su thought recess was the most fun. It was great to have so many friends. Su Su just knew if she could only play ball, with the boys, she could win the game with a homerun.

When school was out there were patrol boys to help the students across the street and on the bus. It had been a big day for Su Su, one she would long remember. It was the starting of an interesting and new adventure in learning. She would soon be reading and writing. Through reading she would become acquainted with a whole new wide world and millions of people in lands she has never seen.

Sun Night
Sept 17, 1961

Dear Susie,

It is time to visit for a little while with you. Next week I hope it will be me you are looking for on Tues. instead of a letter. It will be nice to see you again and to get a report first hand on your school activities. I wonder if you have had to wear your new school coat? We were glad to hear Markie had a new one too. It won't be long before it will soon be winter.

There is a squirrel that has a nest in the tree where we have the bird house. He has been gathering walnuts from a tree next door and carrying them to his nest. He is getting ready for winter. Also there are fewer birds around, I am sure some of them have already started south for the winter.

Hope to see you soon.

Love and kisses,
Granbill
Sunday Eve
Oct 1 '61

Sun Night
Oct 29 '61

Dear Susie,

I heard you were going to have company today; your Grandad and Grandmother Emery.

I am sure you enjoyed seeing them and I know they were glad to see you.

Was Markie happy to get home? I know it must have been lonesome for you without him. It has sure been quiet around here since he left, and we have missed him. Tell him the squirrel took all the pecans that we put out for it. It must be putting them away in its freezer for eating later. Of course the squirrel's freezer would be a hole in the tree that he could get into when it gets cold. That way he wouldn't have to look for food in the snow.

Hope you have fun "Treak or Treatin". We have candy and apples all ready for the little goblins that will be ringing our door bell and when they come we will be thinking of you.

Love and kisses,
Granbill

There is one thing Su Su learned, and that is you can't always play and work at the same time. She learned this one time when she was helping Mommie with the dishes, and Markie came running in wanting to play, when he bumped into her the dishes crashed to the floor and it was more work sweeping up the pieces.

Su Su rides a school bus to school. Some of the kids try to play on it, they push and shove and the bus driver has to tell them to be quiet, so they won't hurt themselves or someone else. He doesn;t have to scold Su Su though, she sits quiet, because she has learned there is a time to be quiet, a time to work and a time to play.

Mommie is waiting. She thinks it is much harder than Su Su's waiting for Santa Clause, for she is waiting for a new baby. She hopes it gets here before Santa makes his rounds.

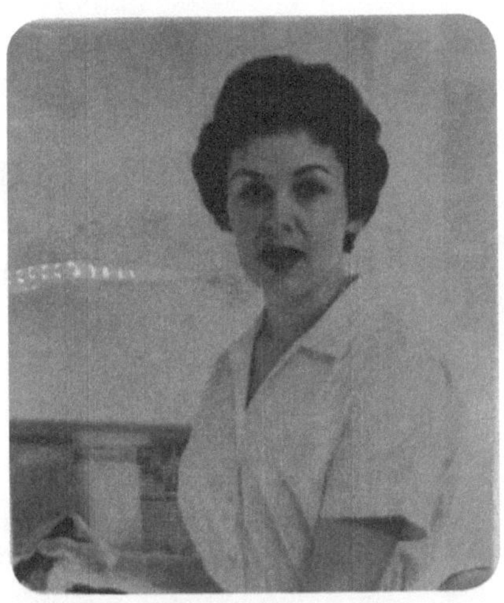

Grammie is also waiting. She has her bags all packed waiting to catch a bus for Su Su's house just as soon as Daddy calls saying the baby is here or on the way. All the waiting and excitement is hard for Su Su, Markie, Mommie and Grammie, but the excitement of a new baby and christmas, will make them forget all the waiting and anxious moments.

Su Su Has A New Little Brother

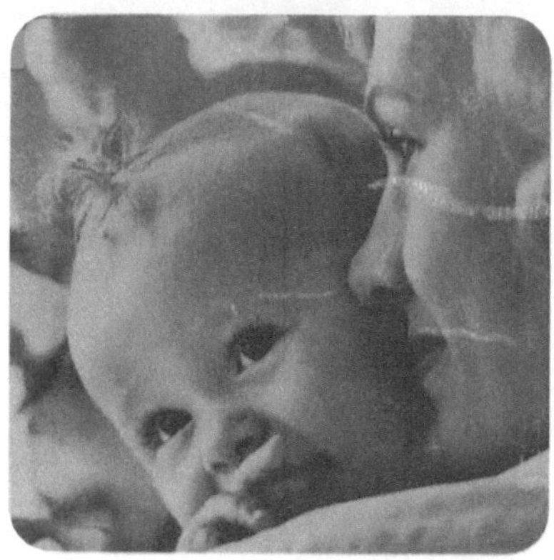

Su Su had waited a long time for her new little brother. It had seemed ages since Mommie first told Su Su they were to have a new baby. As the last day arrived no one could have been more thrilled than Su Su with her new little brother.

When Su Su first learned about the baby she thought it would be nice to have a little sister. As she grew up Su Su could teach her girl games and all the things little girls need to learn, even sewing and knitting.

Markie had hoped for a little brother to grow up with. They could play boy games. They would become great pals, fishing, hunting and playing ball together. Because Markie and the baby would be nearer the same age, Su Su could see why it was the best he was a boy. Su Su, being older will be able to help watch over and guide both her little brother Markie as they grow.

Su Su and Markie think they are very lucky to have such a fine little brother but the new baby Micheal is just as fortunate to have been born into such a fine family as he will have Su Su, Markie, Mommie and Daddy.

www.ingramcontent.com/pod-product-compliance
Lightning Source LLC
Chambersburg PA
CBHW032303070726

47590CB00015B/290